Once Upon A Time At The Adelphi

A musical by
Phil Willmott

With additional music and arrangements by
Elliot Davis

Samuel French — London
www.samuelfrench-london.co.uk

Copyright © 2012 by Phil Willmott (Book, Music and Lyrics)
and Elliot Davis (Additional Music and Arrangements)
All Rights Reserved

ONCE UPON A TIME AT THE ADELPHI is fully protected under the copyright laws of the British Commonwealth, including Canada, the United States of America, and all other countries of the Copyright Union. All rights, including professional and amateur stage productions, recitation, lecturing, public reading, motion picture, radio broadcasting, television and the rights of translation into foreign languages are strictly reserved.

ISBN 978-0-573-18020-0
www.samuelfrench.co.uk
www.samuelfrench.com

For Amateur Production Enquiries

United Kingdom and World excluding North America

plays@samuelfrench.co.uk
020 7255 4302/01

Each title is subject to availability from Samuel French, depending upon country of performance.

CAUTION: Professional and amateur producers are hereby warned that ONCE UPON A TIME AT THE ADELPHI is subject to a licensing fee. Publication of this play does not imply availability for performance. Both amateurs and professionals considering a production are strongly advised to apply to the appropriate agent before starting rehearsals, advertising, or booking a theatre. A licensing fee must be paid whether the title is presented for charity or gain and whether or not admission is charged.

All professional rights whatsoever in this play, its music and songs, are strictly reserved and application for professional performance, etc., should be made before rehearsals to Micheline Steinberg Associates, 104 Great Portland Street, London W1W 6PE www.steinplays.com (email: info@steinplays.com). No performance/presentation of any kind may be given unless a licence has been obtained.

No one shall make any changes in this title for the purpose of production. No part of this book may be reproduced, stored in a retrieval system, or transmitted in any form, by any means, now known or yet to be invented, including mechanical, electronic, photocopying, recording, videotaping, or otherwise, without the prior written permission of the publisher. No one shall upload this title, or part of this title, to any social media websites.

The right of Phil Willmott to be identified as writer and composer of this work with additional music and arrangements by Elliot Davis has been asserted by them in accordance with Section 77 of the Copyright, Designs and Patents Act 1988.

Cover design incorporates a photograph by Rept0n1x, via Wikimedia Commons

ONCE UPON A TIME AT THE ADELPHI

Commissioned by Liverpool Everyman and Playhouse and first performed at the Liverpool Playhouse on 28th June 2008 with the following cast:

Thompson	Simon Bailey
Jo and **Young Alice**	Julie Atherton
Older Alice and **Mo**	Natasha Searle
Babs and **Delores**	Helen Carter
Lord Rothmore etc.	Neil McCaul
Roy Rogers etc.	Nick Smithers
Fritz and **Frank** etc.	Tom Oakley

With Lisa Clifford, Sophie Edwards, Victoria Inez Hardy, Michael Ledwich, Kane Murray, Sally Peerless, Jennifer Riley, Jennifer Thornton

Directed by Phil Willmott
Musical Direction by Elliot Davis
Choreography by Andrew Wright
Design by Christopher Woods
Lighting Design by Ben Cracknell
Sound Design by Jason Barnes
Assistant Director Joe Fredericks

Subsequently produced at the Union Theatre, London in March 2010 by Holly Reiss and Joe Fredericks for Mokita Grit Productions in association with the Steam Industry. The cast included:

Thompson	Jon-Paul Hevey
Jo and **Young Alice**	Rebecca Hutchinson
Babs	Jamie Birkett
Delores	Lucyelle Cliffe
Older Alice	Ally Holmes
Mo	Jodie Michaels
Neil	Matt Markwick
Fritz	Will Stokes
Carlos and **Frank**	Marc Antolin
Roy Rogers	Matthew Naegeli
Lord Rothmore	Paddy Crawley

With Emma Barr, Joanna Goodwin, Lucinda Lawrence, Lindsay Scigliano, Emily Barlow, Nicholas Collier, Benjamin Bond, Rudi Last

Directed by Phil Willmott
Set Design by Charlie Cridlan
Costume Design by Geraldine Spencer
Choreography by Andrew Wright
Musical direction by Michael Bradley
Musical Supervisor Elliot Davis
Lighting Designer Steve Miller

CHARACTERS

Neil Ashby, employee from the present Adelphi Hotel
Jo, employee from the present Adelphi Hotel
Young Alice Summers, employee from the past Adelphi Hotel
Older Alice Summers, from the past
Mo, Thompson's mum from the past
Hollywood's Delores Gilmore, from the past
Thompson, from the past
Lord Rothmore, from the past
Older Thompson, from the past
Algernon Lamb, a 1930s Adelphi Hotel guest
Paddy, a 1930s kitchen porter
Carlos Gardel, 1930s Hollywood Tango star
Frank, from 1930s London
Gwendolyn DeVere, 1930s Adelphi Hotel guest
Babs Barlow, a Liverpudlian maid in 1930s Adelphi Hotel
Fritz, a German 1930s kitchen porter
Henry DeVere, a 1930s Adelphi Hotel guest
Matthew Tremain, a 1930s Adelphi Hotel guest
Henri, a French 1930s kitchen porter
Roy Rogers, 1930s Hollywood cowboy star
Brad Finkle, a 1940s American G.I.
Her Ladyship, a 1930s Adelphi Hotel guest
Druscilla, her daughter, a 1930s Adelphi Hotel guest
Older Babs, in the 1940s
Henry DeVere, a 1930s Adelphi Hotel guest
First Russian Acrobat
Second Russian Acrobat
Fred, a 1930s Adelphi Hotel bell boy
Rose, a 1930s Adelphi Hotel maid
Dorothy, a 1930s Adelphi Hotel maid
Lilly, a 1930s Adelphi Hotel maid
Adelphi Hotel Guests, from the past and present, **Dancers, Russian Acrobats**

Please see page xi for cast ages and suggested doubling

SYNOPSIS OF SCENES

ACT I
SCENE 1 The Adelphi Hotel reception. The present
SCENE 2 The Adelphi roof. Soon afterwards
         An Adelphi reception room. The past
SCENE 3 Mo's house in a working-class area of Liverpool. The past
         The Adelphi roof. The past and present
         The Adelphi Hotel reception. The present
SCENE 4 The Adelphi kitchen. 1930s
         The Adelphi Hotel reception. 1930s
SCENE 5 The Adelphi entrance. 1930s
SCENE 6 The Adelphi ballroom. That night
SCENE 7 The Adelphi roof. The past

ACT II
SCENE 1 The Adelphi roof. The present
         The Accounts Department. The past
SCENE 2 The Adelphi Hotel reception. The past
SCENE 3 An Adelphi bedroom. The past
SCENE 4 The Adelphi Hotel reception. The past
SCENE 5 The Adelphi roof. The past
SCENE 6 The Adelphi Hotel reception. The past (and briefly the present)
         Mo's house. The past
SCENE 7 The Adelphi ballroom. The past
SCENE 8 Telephones at the Adelphi Hotel and in Germany. The past
SCENE 9 The Adelphi ballroom. The past, it's a month later
SCENE 10 The Adelphi roof. The past and present

The action takes place in the Adelphi Hotel, Liverpool

Time—the present, 1930s and 1940s

MUSICAL NUMBERS

No. 1   Overture

ACT I

No. 1A	Jo and Neil underscore	
No. 2	Somebody's on the Roof	**Neil, Jo, Hotel Guests**
No. 3	Thompson	**Older Alice**
No. 3A	After Thompson underscore	
No. 4	Once in a Lifetime	**Lord Rothmore, Thompson, Young Alice**
No. 4A	Into Mo's House underscore	
No. 4B	Thompson's Prospect underscore	
No. 5	First Romances	**Mo**
No. 5A	Into Kitchens underscore	
No. 6	Musical Comedy Showtune	**Thompson, Kitchen Staff**
No. 6A	Fritz underscore	
No. 7	Rats	**Fritz, Thompson**
No. 7A	Harassment underscore	
No. 8	Red Carpet Rolldown	
No. 9	A Wedding and a Yacht	**Babs, Men**
No. 10	Cocktail Party	
No. 11	Yippee Ai Eh!	**Roy Rogers, Babs**
No. 12	Tell Her	**Thompson, Babs, Young Alice, Fritz**
No. 13	Act I Finale	**Babs, Young Alice, Ensemble**

ACT II

No. 14	Entr'acte	
No. 14A	Alice Reappears underscore	
No. 15	Thompson from Accounts	**Girls, Thompson, Boys, Older Alice, Britannia**
No. 16	Tell Them	**Babs, Thompson**
No. 17	Bedroom underscore	
No. 18	Dance For Me, Boy	**Dolores Gilmore**
No. 18A	Transition to Act II, Scene 4	
No. 19	The Next Ten Seconds	**Young Alice**

No. 19A	Neil's Next Ten Seconds	**Neil**
No. 19B	Young Alice's Next Ten Seconds (Reprise)	**Young Alice**
No. 20	Take a Moment	**Thompson, Young Alice**
No. 21	Just Fine	**Young Alice, Older Alice**
No. 22	Dance For Me, Boy (Reprise)	**G.I.s, Babs, Girls, Brad, Ensemble**
No. 23	Tell Him	**Older Alice**
No. 23A	Telegram into Bombing	
No. 24	Act II Finale, Once in a Lifetime (Reprise)	**Jo, Alice, Neil, Thompson, Ensemble**
No. 25	First Bows	
No. 25A	Bows Part II	

The score and associated orchestral parts are available on hire from Samuel French Ltd.

Dedication

To all performers, creatives and technicians who've helped the show develop through the various incarnations of *Once Upon a Time at the Adelphi* and the US version, *Once Upon a Time in Atlantic City*

PRODUCTION NOTES

STAGING ONCE UPON A TIME AT THE ADELPHI

I was lucky enough to get the chance to direct the show twice over an eighteen-month period, in a spectacular premiere at the Playhouse Theatre in Liverpool and in an equally successful, simply staged, studio production at the Union Theatre in London.

The first benefitted from a stunning, award-nominated set by Christopher Woods in which an elegant, gold, interlinking framework of skeletal elements from the hotel, mounted on two concentric revolves, span each setting magically into view including staircases taking actors to various levels.

In contrast Charlie Cridlan designed a bold, simple and dramatic set for our London run in which she imagined what the Adelphi Hotel sign would look like if you stood behind it on the roof of the building. The top half of the back of the individual A, D, E, L, P, H and I stood waist height from the floor and the actors moved amongst them throughout, relating to them as furniture (countertops, doorways etc.) when appropriate or as a background to the rooftop action during scenes on top of the hotel.

Both approaches perfectly suited the contrasting venues and your theatre will be different too, so you'll notice that there are very few stage directions in the script relating to scenery, as the musical can be mounted in so many different ways.

For instance, at the end of the first number when Jo goes out on to the hotel roof you can either choose a change of scenery or simply cross fade to a different lighting state with a gentle wind sound effect, as the ensemble leave the stage, parting to reveal Older Alice; letting the dialogue do the work for you.

Once Older Alice starts to tell her story we're watching her memories. Like a memory the action should move easily from one location to the next as fluidly as possible, so a shift in light and sound and minimal set change is always preferable to holding up the action whilst you trundle on cumbersome scenic elements. Furniture should be minimal.

In my productions Older Alice stayed on stage throughout observing the action. This also helped the audience understand they were watching flashbacks of her memories.

I have always had the actress playing Jo also play Alice's younger self in these flashbacks but I recently saw a production where the roles were separated and if you've a large cast, that can work equally well.

Sometimes the actor playing Neil also plays Younger Thompson which works nicely when Jo is Younger Alice too but, however you double the lovers, by the end we need to see Jo dance with Neil and an Older Alice dance with an Older Thompson for maximum emotional impact.

CAST

The following is a suggested doubling for a company of 7 principals and an additional dance ensemble of 4. (It is desirable although not essential for Jo to double with Young Alice and Neil to double with Thompson)

Jo from today's Adelphi Hotel / **Young Alice** from the past
(Female age 20s)

Older Alice Summers from the past / **Mo**, Thompson's mum from the past / **Hollywood's Delores Gilmore** from the past
(Female age 40s)

Neil Ashby from today's Adelphi Hotel / **Thompson from the past** / and as cast.
(Male age 20s)

Guest in today's Adelphi Hotel / **Lord Rothmor**e from the past / **Older Thompson** / and as cast.
(Male age 40s)

Guest in today's Adelphi Hotel / **Algernon Lamb**, a 1930s Adelphi Hotel Guest / **Paddy**, a 1930s Kitchen Porter / Hollywood's Tango Star **Carlos Gardel** / **Frank** from London / **Male Dancer** in Overture Dance, Show Tune, Wedding and a Yacht, Thompson from Accounts, Boogie Woogie dance routine (from Dance for Me, Boy (Reprise))
(Male age 20/30s)

Guest in today's Adelphi Hotel / **Gwendolyn DeVere**, a 1930s Adelphi Hotel Guest / **Babs Barlow**, a Liverpudlian Maid in 1930s Adelphi Hotel / **Female Dancer** in Overture Dance, Show Tune, Thompson from Accounts, Boogie Woogie dance routine (from Dance for Me, Boy (Reprise))
(Female age 20s)

Fritz from the past / **Henry DeVere**, a 1930s Adelphi Hotel Guest / **Male Dancer** in Overture Dance, Show Tune, Wedding and a Yacht, Thompson from Accounts and Boogie Woogie dance routine (from Dance for Me, Boy (Reprise)), and as cast.
(Male age 20s)

Guest in today's Adelphi Hotel / Matthew Tremain, a 1930s Adelphi Hotel Guest / **Henri**, a 1930s kitchen porter / Hollywood's cowboy star **Roy Rogers / Brad Finkle**, a G.I. / **Male Dancer** in Overture Dance, Show Tune, Wedding and a Yacht, Thompson from Accounts and Boogie Woogie dance routine (from Dance for Me, Boy (Reprise)), and as cast. (Male age 20/30s)

Guest in today's Adelphi Hotel / Her Ladyship, a 1930s Adelphi Hotel Guest / **Older Babs / Ensemble Female Dancer** in Overture Dance, Show Tune, Wedding and a Yacht, Thompson from Accounts, Boogie Woogie dance routine (from Dance for Me, Boy (Reprise)), and as cast. (Female age 40+)

Ensemble Roles:
Henry DeVere, a 1930s Adelphi Hotel Guest / **First Russian Acrobat**
Fred, a 1930s bell boy / **Second Russian Acrobat**
Rose, a 1930s hotel maid / **Druscilla**, a 1930s hotel guest
Dorothy, a 1930s hotel maid
Who also serve as:
Dancers in Overture Dance, Show Tune, Wedding and a Yacht, Thompson from Accounts, Boogie Woogie dance routine (from Dance for Me, Boy (Reprise)) / **Russian Acrobats / Guests in today's Adelphi Hotel**

Plus:
Additional Dancers, Covers and Swings as required in Overture Dance, Show Tune, Wedding and a Yacht, Thompson from Accounts, Boogie Woogie dance routine (from Dance for Me, Boy (Reprise)).

PHIL WILLMOTT

MORE REVIEWS OF ONCE UPON A TIME AT THE ADELPHI

"This is that frighteningly rare thing: an entirely original new British musical, not based on a pre-existing film story and/or existing pop catalogue, receiving its premiere by a regional producing theatre. The result? A musical that has arrived at the Liverpool Playhouse that is actually ready for proper public exposure," Mark Shenton, *Stage Online*

"Phil Willmott's vividly characterised, poignantly told and appealingly tuneful show is original and the best new musical to hail from the city since *Blood Brothers*." *Sunday Express*

"A remarkable achievement. A fluid line-up of song and dance numbers, with an MGM verve and velocity." *Independent*

"A fabulous new musical fairy tale for the year 2008. A thoroughly enjoyable evening. It was refreshing to hear the new music — which left everyone in the audience with smiles on their faces." *Theatreworld*

"Willmott knows how to pen a tune... 'Once In A Lifetime', whose swelling melody is hot-wired directly to the tear-ducts, should be designated the official anthem of the Capital of Culture." *Guardian*

"The music is sweeping and grandiose and the songs themselves are catchy." *What's On Stage*

"Immensely enjoyable ... A show to warm Liverpool hearts ... raised a storm of approval from a packed house." *Chester Chronicle*

"Phil Willmott's determinedly feel-good show. His piece has a celebratory air suited to the buoyancy that the title of European City of Culture seems to have brought to Liverpool ... Such joyous moments are the musical's strength." *The Times*

"*Once Upon a Time at the Adelphi* is worth seeing ... Like a bottle of vintage Krug, there is an awful lot of fizz with Phil Willmott's musical." *Stage*

"A triumph of staging. The place that transformed popular music with its boldness here defines itself with nostalgia ..." *Observer*

Other plays by Phil Willmott published by
Samuel French Ltd

The Adventures of Jason and the Argonauts
Around the World in Eighty Days
Lysistrata — The Sex Strike (with Germaine Greer)

ACT I

The Adelphi Hotel, Liverpool

No. 1 Overture

A big brassy overture plays whilst onstage action contrasts the Adelphi Hotel, Liverpool then and now. In the original production characters from the present walked past a mirror and were reflected by the identical movements of parallel characters from the past

Scene 1

The Adelphi reception. The present day

No. 1A Jo and Neil underscore

Neil approaches Jo. They are both young and dressed for reception work

Jo There you are, I've been worried about you — you're late, posh boy.
Neil I'm allowed to be late on my last day. Jo, I want you to come to Japan with me.
Jo So you said last night. Now, the queue out at reception's like Primark on a Saturday.

Introduction to "Somebody's on the Roof" starts

Get some guests booked in and checked out and we'll talk about this later.
Neil Battle stations!

The Lights and set change to the Adelphi front desk

They're swamped by present day Guests, played by the company, at the Adelphi front desk, all trying to get their attention

The hubbub segues into:

No. 2 Somebody's on the Roof

Guests of various types sing

Hen Party Girls	What time's breakfast?
Football Supporters	
(*glaring at each other*)	When do I check out?
American Husband	Is the Cavern far?
Sheik	Where is Aintree?
Backpacker	Anfield? Kirkby?
American Wife	I wanna meet Ringo Star.
Business Woman	My company booked this.
Liverpool Supporter	I'm on your guest list.
Chav Husband	The room's too hot.
Chav Wife	I'm cold.
Everton Supporter	So we're not near Albert Dock here?

Neil (*speaking on the phone*) Adelphi Hotel. Please hold. (*He puts the receiver to one side*)

Business Woman	Where's John Lennon Airport?
Hen Party Girl 1	Can you fly to Magaluf?

Neil listens to the phone again

Hen Party Girl 2   My earring stud's gone missing

Neil (*speaking into the phone*) Who's this?

(*Singing to Jo*)   Somebody's on the roof.

When Jo sings to herself, Neil and the aggravated Guests go into slow motion, returning to normal speed each time she finishes

Jo (*to herself*)   Why'd he tell me all that stuff?
Losing him was bad enough.

Why'd he kiss me?
Why'd he do that?
Did he mean what he said?
Maybe I was hoping
But this is like eloping
Is he soft in the head?

Act I, Scene 1

All right, yes, he's
Kind of dishy
But he's also me mate.
Come on, girl, give over —
Him as Casanova?
Us on a date?

Yet when he chucked his job in
To leave this place for good
Why'd I bawl my eyes out
Like a lover would?
Stop it —
Working here is fun
You can't just give up and run.

All Guests	What time's breakfast?
	When do I check out?
Jo (*to herself*)	Why are they so rude?
Business Woman	Where's my taxi?
Everton Supporter	Sandwich?
Backpacker	Room key?
Jo (*to herself*)	Grumpy, thick or crude?
Business Woman	My company booked this
Sheik	I'm on your guest list
American Wife	Our room is cold
American Husband	No, hot!
Jo (*to herself*)	I'm a person with a name,
	Can't you read or what?!
(*To Neil*)	If they don't stop their moaning
	I'll kill 'em that's the truth.
Guests	Can we get some service here ——

Neil (*speaking, still on the phone*) There's somebody on the roof.

Jo (*singing, to herself*)	Why'd he kiss me?
	Why'd he do that?
	Did he mean what he said?
Guests	'Scuse me I'm waiting here!
Jo (*to herself*)	Why'd he get all heavy?
	Just met him for a bevy
	Now he's messed with me head.
	All right, yes, it's
	Kind of tempting

Guests	Me and him in Japan.
	Oi love, you deaf or what?!
Jo (*to herself*)	But I don't speak the lingo
	Who'd drive our nan to bingo?
	And I'm no sushi fan.

Neil (*speaking to Jo*) The caller says she might jump. (*Into the phone*) Who *is* this?

Jo (*to herself*)	I love the Adelphi
	Each corner of here
	Should I leave here 'cause some fella
	Stuck his fat tongue in my ear?
(*Slow*)	Though his kisses thrill me
	I need a sign, some proof
	That leaving here's the right thing ——

Neil (*speaking*) Jo!

Guests (*singing*)	Can we get some service please?
Neil (*singing to Jo*)	There's somebody on the roof!
Guests	What time's breakfast? When do I check out?
Neil	There's somebody on the roof!

The number resolves

Segue to Playout for scene change music

Scene 2

The roof of the Adelphi. Present day, soon afterwards. A reception room in the Adelphi. The past

Jo approaches the Older Alice who's standing in shadow

Jo You all right, love? It's a bit cold up here, isn't it?
Older Alice Is it? I don't notice. The roof has always been my favourite place in the whole hotel. When I used to work here.
Jo You worked here?
Older Alice For many years. Back in the old days.
Jo Look, let's go down, eh? Heights do me head in.

Older Alice Ah but that's part of it. He used to say up here is like real life but with extra danger to keep things interesting. Anything can happen. We all thought we had Adolf Hitler up here once. And a horse.
Jo A horse! Adolf Hit — On the roof of the Adelphi?! Somebody once told me that Hitler once worked here and something about a cowboy but it's all just a myth. Look, let's get you inside.
Older Alice But I've got an appointment.
Jo Up here?
Older Alice Someone very special.
Jo Are you sure? I mean … There's a lot of stairs once the lift stops.
Older Alice Thompson always makes that little extra effort. We got together up here and once made a pact that we would always mark our anniversary with a little dance and a glass of champagne on this roof. And so this is where you'll find me, every year at this time, waiting for him.

The intro to "Thompson" starts

Jo (*kindly*) I don't think there's anyone coming up here tonight, love.
Older Alice Oh he'll be here, Thompson always makes an effort. It was the 1930s and … (*She sings*)

No. 3 Thompson

> He was so beautiful
> The way he'd part his hair
> He was so beautiful,
> When I saw him standing there

As the music swells she steps out of the shadows. She is an attractive woman in her early forties, dressed in a smart 1940 coat that would still look classy today

> The years simply fell away
> I remembered him, from school you see,
> It seemed like yesterday.

Flashback

Young Thompson appears. A handsome and charismatic young man with a slightly roguish air. He approaches Young Alice, a pretty young woman whose dark, reserved dress suggests she's a hotel employee. Young Alice can be doubled with Jo

High society guests begin to fill the stage around them. Half the company play guests, the other half will appear as hotel staff. Amongst them is the hotel's new owner, Lord Henry Rothmore, the newly-married Henry and Gwendolyn DeVere, Her Ladyship, and the financiers Algernon Lamb and Matthew Tremain. The Guests hold glasses

> And when he noticed me
> His smile, just sort of beamed
> I didn't stand a chance
> Or so it seemed.
> He was mine, I was his for ever more.
> Would I have run
> If I'd have known
> The trouble I'd in store?

Thompson addresses Young Alice. He often uses an elegant turn of phrase which indicates his high society aspirations

Thompson Ladybird?
Older Alice (*lost in her memories*) Tommy Thompson.
Young Alice What are you doing here? I mean your mum told us you were still studying. University. With the nobs.
Thompson That didn't work out. Haven't quite managed to tell Ma.
Young Alice No! It'll break her heart ... the scholarship, the ...
Thompson I'll still make her proud. Just got to work out where I fit in. Too Dingle for university and I'll wager I'm too university for Dingle now.
Young Alice (*sending him up*) Oh, you'll "wager" will you? You've certainly come along way from the gobshite who used to get my brother into trouble.
Thompson If only he knew how much I adored his earnest little sister in the ladybird red coat.
Young Alice Lost your accent but none of your cheek.

The events unfold as described. Throughout the following, Thompson works the room, charming the Guests and gaining their confidence

Older Alice (*singing*) He was so charming then,
> You didn't stand a chance.
> When Thompson called the tune
> The world would dance.
> One wink and he always made you feel

Act I, Scene 2

>No one else was there but you
>A quite unique appeal.
>Men would seek his friendship
>By the score,
>Their wives would smile
>And dream of something more.
>So confident
>He drew the world's applause
>His manner quite disguising all
>The chaos he could cause.

Young Alice regains Thompson's attention

Young Alice What are you doing here?
Thompson Following up a few business leads. There's a lot of money here tonight. The new Lord Rothmore's hoping to attract investors to expand the hotel. He's a lot more ambitious than his father.
Young Alice You in business now then?
Thompson That's enough about me. What's become of you?
Young Alice I'm a housekeeper here at the Adelphi.
Thompson Haven't we both done well?
Young Alice Oh this is nothing compared to you.
Thompson We've both come a long way from Empire Road Infants.
Young Alice So what line of business are you in?
Thompson Financial management.

Thompson moves off. Older Alice describes what we see next

Older Alice (*singing*) The signs were there
>I should have run a mile
>But by then he'd trapped me with his smile.
>I watched as he chose his latest prey.
>Perhaps I should have warned the man
>But then what could I say?
>Thompson wandered idly to his side
>And praised him on his recent choice of bride.
>Dazzled by such easy charm and self-belief
>No one ever spotted
>Thompson also was a thief.

On the word "thief" Young Alice notices Thompson, unobserved by anyone else, throw a pocket-watch in the air, catch it and slip it into his pocket

The song ends and the music segues to underscoring

The Guests at the vintage party become very agitated

Matthew Tremain Great heavens. My wallet. My wallet's missing! Check your wallet, Algy.
Algernon Lamb My pocket's been picked too! By Jove how on earth ––
Her Ladyship My bracelet!
Henry DeVere My watch. Rothmore. My pocket-watch is missing.
Lord Rothmore Oh dear. Mine too.

They all suddenly notice and turn on Young Alice. Thompson ducks down to hide

Her Ladyship Girl! You must call the police at once!
Matthew Tremain I demand an explanation!
Algernon Lamb This is a disgrace!
Lord Rothmore Mr Lamb … Most unfortunate. I can assure you ––
Her Ladyship The girl's an idiot. Rothmore, call the police! There's a pickpocket at large.
Lord Rothmore Your Ladyship, I cannot apologize enough I ––
Gwendolyn DeVere We'll all have our throats slit next! Henry!
Henry DeVere Gwendolyn, do keep calm. The police! Henry, you really must call the police at once!
Lord Rothmore (*to Young Alice*) Miss Summers would you mind?
Young Alice Certainly, sir. I'll call them at once.

"Thompson" underscore out

(*Aside; whispering urgently to Thompson*) You. Up the back stairs to the roof now.

Fred, the bell boy, approaches Young Alice

Thompson ducks aside to avoid detection

Fred Everything all right, Miss S?
Young Alice Perfectly thank you, Fred.

Fred moves off

(*Bundling Thompson out*) Don't talk to anyone. The shame of this'd kill your mum.

Act I, Scene 2

Thompson Ladybird, I shall never pull your pigtails again.

Thompson exits

No. 3A "After Thompson" underscore starts

The flashback fades away and the Lights focus down on Jo and Older Alice

Older Alice So you see. Up here was where it all started.
Jo Didn't you tell him to sling his hook? He could have lost you your job.
Older Alice Oh I wanted to, but the 1930s were exciting times. the First World War seemed a distant nightmare, people were saying the recession was over, old Lord Rothmore had passed away and his young son had big plans for this place. Somehow Thompson had a way of tapping in to all that.

"Thompson" underscore out

Guests reassemble as Lord Rothmore prepares to address them in the reception room

Announcer Pray silence for Lord Rothmore.
Lord Rothmore Your Ladyship, ladies and gentlemen, friends. I'm informed the police will be here very shortly to take statements and of course I shall make good any losses you may have incurred at my hotel. Twice over. For I want you all to be happy. Tonight we stand on the eve of a great adventure.

"Once in a Lifetime" underscore begins

    Liverpool has been through some terrible times of late but I believe we are turning the corner. We cannot be downtrodden for long, for man is a noble beast that can and will always survive life's setbacks.

The action and lighting alternates between Lord Rothmore in the hotel reception room and Thompson and Young Alice on the roof. The underscoring switches back and forth between Lord Rothmore's music and a softer theme on the roof

Young Alice All right, hand it all over.
Thompson Ladybird ——

Young Alice Shut it!

Young Alice holds out her hand. He surrenders a wallet

And the rest.

The underscoring switches

As Lord Rothmore continues speaking in the reception room, up on the roof Thompson divests himself of an amazing amount of loot from various pockets and Young Alice puts it all in a bag

Lord Rothmore For we are opportunists. We cannot pass by when a chance to replenish our coffers presents itself. Nor should we. It is the pioneering spirit that made this city great and it is pioneers that will make us great again.

The underscoring switches. Thompson seems to have finished but Young Alice glares at him

Young Alice And the rest.

And he surrenders one more wallet

Thank you. Now I'll send this lot down in the dumb waiter.
Thompson (*showing off*) Thank you for showing such compassion to an old friend on his uppers. How do I effect an escape?
Young Alice (*sending him up*) You don't. Effect a move from this spot before I get back and I'll chin you.
Thompson Alice.
Young Alice What?

He hands over a final wallet

Young Alice leaves

Thompson stares out at the view. The underscoring changes and we switch back to Lord Rothmore

Lord Rothmore Are we to stay mired in our current difficulties? No. Our commercial ambitions must fly once more to the far flung corners of the earth. As past city leaders looked to the trade routes of Ceylon and China, and the Indies to supply the produce on which our past

Act I, Scene 2   11

wealth was founded so we at this hotel will look beyond our shores for a commodity *we* can import. Ladies and gentlemen. We will import — Hollywood.

The music swells

The motion picture industry is reaching across the Atlantic like never before. Britain wants to meet its stars and the great ocean liners will deliver those stars to Liverpool docks. We need to build a hotel here, so splendid that the gods and goddesses of the silver screen will regard us as the only possible port of call on their way to meet the people of Britain. Ladies and gentlemen, I cannot finance this alone but with your investment the Adelphi could be fit for Hollywood, and the eyes of the world will envy us once more. (*He sings, anthem-like*)

No. 4 Once in a Lifetime (1)

> The stars are calling out our name
> It's Liverpool's time again
> At last the world is waking.
> Shout the news across the sky
> Tonight it's you and I
> Who'll choose the road we're taking.
>
> For tonight
> If we dream
> The world will dream along with us.
> We've waited long enough, now is the right time.
> If we fail then we fail but at least we chose to fight
> Don't waste tonight's
> Once in a lifetime.

Young Alice bustles back to Thompson on the roof

The underscore continues

Young Alice Right, just what the bloody hell do you think you're playing at, mister? Our whole street looked up to you. The first one of us to get out, the first one of us to go to university. When you won that scholarship it was like it was for all of us. How dare you throw all that away ——
Thompson Shut up.
Young Alice (*furiously*) You what?

Thompson Sorry, I mean just be quiet, just for a minute. Listen.

Music out

Young Alice I can't hear anything.
Thompson No? I don't believe that.

The underscore comes back in

We're high above Liverpool in the moonlight on a perfect clear midnight. Do you really want to waste this moment fighting? The city's spread out before us like gems on a bed of black velvet, so beautiful it takes your breath away and in the silence — (*He sings, gently at first*)

> The stars are calling out our name
> It's Liverpool's time again
> At last the world is waking.
> Shout the news across the sky
> Tonight it's you and I
> Who'll choose the road we're taking.
>
> For tonight
> If we dream
> The world will dream along with us.
> We've waited long enough, now is the right time.
> If we fail then we fail but at least we chose to fight
> Don't waste tonight's
> Once in a lifetime.

The music swells during the following

Lord Rothmore Thank you for your support, friends, I knew I could count on you. Tonight, thanks to your generosity, Liverpool's recovery begins. Tomorrow we will begin recruiting new staff, the ordinary men and women of Liverpool, of Ireland, of the poor countries of Europe — if they will work hard and share our vision we will take them in. For it is their dedication alone that will make your dreams a reality. (*Raising his glass*) Ladies and gentlemen, I give you the noble staff of the Adelphi Hotel.

Hotel staff enter the reception room and stand in attendance

Back on the roof, Young Alice sings

Act I, Scene 3

Young Alice The stars are calling out our name
It's Liverpool's time again
At last the world is waking
Young Alice ⎫ Shout the news across the sky
⎬ Tonight it's you and I
Who'll choose the road we're taking.
Ensemble ⎭ Ah ... Ah ... Ah ... taking.

All For tonight
If we dream
The world will dream along with us,
We've waited long enough, now is the right time
If we fail then we fail but at least we chose to fight
Don't waste tonight's
Once in a lifetime.

Big finish. The reception Guests slowly raise their glasses towards the audience in a toast

Don't waste tonight's
Once in a lifetime.

Scene change music No. 4A "Into Mo's House"

Scene 3

Mo's house in Dingle, a working-class area of Liverpool; the past. The Adelphi roof; past and present. Adelphi reception; present

Thompson visits Mo, his mother. She is hanging out her washing to dry

Thompson Hello, Mam.
Mo Sweet Jesus, you frightened the life out of me. I don't believe it! My boy's come home, come here. (*She hugs him*) I must look a state it's washing day ... if I'd known ——
Thompson You look a million dollars.
Mo My eldest's back. Look at you, handsome, university obviously agrees with you. Why didn't you tell me you were coming?
Thompson Well now, Mam, I like to keep you on your toes.
Mo Listen to you all posh now.
Thompson I'm still Dingle through and through underneath.
Mo How's the studies going?
Thompson Oh I chucked all that in.
Mo What?!

Thompson Yeah Mam, I was gonna tell you university didn't really work out for me. Bit of a square peg in a round hole, tootled off for London a few months ago. In fact, didn't I write and tell you?
Mo I didn't get it.
Thompson Ah, that's the post for you, terrible.
Mo Did you get a job?

Young Alice enters

Young Alice You all right Mrs T?
Mo Alice, you here as well.
Young Alice Can I have a quick word with Thompson?
Mo Yes of course, love. Why don't you both sit down. I'll get you both some tea.

Mo exits shooting an approving look at Young Alice and Thompson. She always hoped they'd get together

Young Alice What would she say if she knew you were a grubby little thief? What made you do it, Thompson?
Thompson I can't get my mind to settle, Alice. It's the danger I love, knowing the whole pack of 'em would turn on you even if they just suspected what you're up to.
Young Alice Sounds like you're proud of it.
Thompson I'm not. I'm not. I know it's wrong. You know how we were brought up but I haven't been able to turn my mind to anything else.
Young Alice Well you're going to now or I'm going to tell the police what I saw tonight. You're in trouble, mister. You've let down every single person that's ever cared about or believed in you.
Thompson No, Alice.
Young Alice You're going to get yourself back on the straight and narrow and you are going to make us all proud. I'm getting you a job at the hotel starting tomorrow.
Thompson (*hopefully*) Doing the books? At the Adelphi?
Young Alice You must be joking. Think I'm going to trust you with the company's money? No way. You've got to prove yourself, prove you're serious about this, and prove you're not afraid of hard work.
Thompson What do I have to do?
Young Alice In the hotel there are dining-rooms. Magnificent food, beautiful surroundings.

No. 4B "Thompson's Prospect" underscore starts

Act I, Scene 3   15

But that's not you. Beneath that are the service stations where the food arrives to be served by immaculate waiters in black and white. Not you. Beneath this are the kitchens where the chefs are gods ruling over an army of chopping, slicing, mixing, making magic. Not you. Beneath that amidst the steam of the ovens in the heat and the dark are the kitchen lads, Irish mostly, but Poles and Frenchies and even Germans sweating away washing pots and heaving crates and the like from dawn till dusk. That's where you're working till you prove you can be trusted.

Underscore out

Thompson I can't be a kitchen porter.
Young Alice Take your choice. It's that or the police. (*Beat*)

Mo returns

Mrs T, I've just got Thompson a job at the Adelphi.
Mo (*delighted*) Oh, Thompson!

Pause

Young Alice Let me know what you decide. (*To Mo*) Me mam sends her best.
Mo See you Sunday, love.

Young Alice exits

I always knew that girl would be the saving of you.
Thompson Mam!

The intro to No. 5 starts

Mo She's always been able to make you see sense when no one else could.
Thompson I'm not some kid with a crush any more. I've got plans.
Mo Of course you have. (*She sings, gently*)

No. 5 First Romances

    Thinking of running away?
    Burying your head in the sand?
    Boy, this is stronger than you

I don't think you understand.
Sometimes we don't have a choice
You'll find the courage you lack
I believe in a map of our lives
That'll always bring you back.

She starts to fold her washing

Love has a way of surviving
First romance, it never disappears
That first kiss you share
The day you were aware
There was another
Who shared your hopes and fears.
Love like that it never really leaves you
The years can never pull you two apart
Though the world can be tough
It's never rough enough
That you'll forget love
The day you let love
In your heart.

She stops folding and hugs a shirt to her

When I think about meeting your dad
Standing there dozy as you
Everyone told me to run
Everyone called me a fool
But I knew I'd found me a man
Who'd stand by me no matter what
And though he's gone I love him still
With every breath I've got.

She and Thompson fold a large sheet between them

Love has a way of surviving
First romance, it never disappears
That first kiss that you share
The day you were aware
There was another
Who shared your hopes and fears.
Love like that it never really leaves you
Years can never pull you two apart

Act I, Scene 3   17

      And though the world can be tough
      It's never rough enough
      That you'll forget love
      The day you let love
      In your heart.
      You don't forget love
      The day you let love
      In your heart.

Mo exits

The Lights change

Young Alice enters

Thompson I'll take the job on one condition.
Young Alice I don't think you're in any position to make demands, mister.
Thompson I'll get a day off, right?
Young Alice One half-day a week.
Thompson Take the same day off as me. I'll do it if I get one afternoon with you a week.
Young Alice You cheeky get. No way.

Thompson exits

Older Alice and Jo alone again

Older Alice But of course I was completely in love with him. I always had been.
Jo How do they do that? People … just … get under your skin like that. One minute you're going along, nice and steady, life kinda OK, job … mates, a few laughs at the weekend and then bang they're looking at you across their third pint like they want to melt your clothes off, and suddenly your heart's in your mouth and you're sweating like a Wag in Harvey Nichols and it turns out people haven't been honest with you and … you wish they had because maybe if you'd realized it earlier it would have been really, really nice, you know, that's what people do to you!

The Lights change to Neil in the modern day hotel reception

Neil (*on the phone*) Jo! Answer your phone can't you, you've been on that roof for half an hour, we need you down here, there's nothing wrong is there? Just some senior took a wrong turn on the stairs, right? Listen, tonight, can we go for a drink? Just give me a chance to convince you ... Japan ... you and me ... we'll be great ... just ... call me back, OK?

Neil exits

The Lights change to Jo and Older Alice on top of the roof

Older Alice People, my dear, or just one special person? (*Back to the story*) They were a tough lot down in the kitchens, where Thompson started work. Just like now it was mostly low-paid immigrants ——

The stage begins to fill with the hustle and bustle of the 1930s Adelphi hotel kitchen with the company as hotel staff

— usually from Ireland and Europe in those days.

Underscoring No. 5a "Into Kitchens" starts

But Thompson soon had them all — porters, chambermaids, bell boys, anyone passing through that kitchen — under his spell.

Scene 4

The Adelphi Hotel kitchen; 1930s. Adelphi reception; 1930s

There are various hotel staff including three kitchen porters, Henri (French), Paddy (Irish) and Fritz (German), and chambermaids, led by Dorothy

Thompson is talking to Fred, the bell boy, who's reading a book amongst the clatter of the kitchens

Thompson You keep up the reading, Fred. I had a shot at university once.

Underscoring out

Fred Really?
Thompson Scholarship and everything. But ... it didn't really work out for me. Bit of a square peg in a round hole. If you study mathematics it soon teaches you to look beyond the ordinary. How could I tie myself

Act I, Scene 4   19

to exams and dry old lectures with it all whizzing round my head? I spun calculations that had those old professors gasping for breath. Soon left 'em lagging behind. London was calling me.
Fred I'd like to go there.
Thompson The only place to be for a brilliant mind.

He's beginning to draw a crowd of interested hotel staff comprising Henri and Paddy and Dorothy and the chambermaids

It would blow you all away. All the sights, all the bustle. I'd have stayed if I hadn't had to come back for Ma.
Fred They say there's lots of opportunity to better yourself.
Henri What happened next?
Thompson I got a job in a cinema.
Fred A picture house.
Dorothy Like the Regal?
Thompson Much bigger, shimmering silver screen the size of a house. We get all the big films first. Your troubles just disappear when the titles roll on the new musical — (*He sings, very bright and breezy*)

No. 6 Musical Comedy Showtune

You can't beat a musical comedy show tune,
A Busby Berkeley matinee.
When Fred Astaire glides on your spirits soar
He'll banish all your blues away.
And soon you're buzzing with the new tune
That's got 'em tapping 'cross the screen.
There's nothing better
To the young go-getter
Than a full-blown
Big time Hollywood dance routine.

Kitchen Staff Member 1 (*speaking*) Hollywood? More like Hollyhead.
Kitchen Staff Member 2 Look at me, I'm Birkenhead. (*He demonstrates some fancy steps*)

Someone else tries, others get caught up

All   You can't beat a musical comedy show tune
                 A Busby Berkeley matinée.
                 Ba ba ba. Da da da da

> When Fred Astaire glides on your spirits soar
> He'll banish all your blues away
> And soon you're buzzing with the new tune (Ah!)
> That's got 'em tapping 'cross the screen.
> Ba ba. Da da!
> There's nothing better
> To the young go-getter
> Than a full-blown
> Big time Hollywood dance routine

The whole thing escalates into a full-blown routine. Tap break, half-time kickline. All the tricks until at the climax everyone's singing

> You can't beat a musical comedy show tune
> A Busby Berkeley matinée
> Ba ba ba. Da da da da
> When Fred Astaire glides on your spirits soar
> He'll banish all your blues away
> And soon you're buzzing with the new tune (Ah!)
> That's got 'em tapping 'cross the screen.
> Ba ba. Da da!
> There's nothing better
> To the young go-getter
> Than a full-blown
> Big time Hollywood —
> Hollywood
> Hollywood
> Hollywood
> Ba ba ba da da da!

Fritz, an intense German youth, interrupts the fun

Fritz (*speaking*) Stop, stop, stop! Can't you see this is just a distraction from the struggle we workers face? In my country the German people starve under the conditions the British and Americans have imposed to crush our spirit

Paddy Fritz mate, cheer up, just this once.

Fritz goes

Thompson You want to get yourself along to the pictures my friend. (*To everyone*) All together now —

Act I, Scene 4   21

All   There's nothing better
                       To the young go-getter

(*Halftime*)   Than a full-blown
                       Big time Hollywood
                       Hollywood
                       Hollywood
                       Hollywood
                       Ba ba ba da da da!
                       Dance
                       ROUTINE!

Black-out

Everyone exits

No. 6A Fritz underscore

The Lights come up on an area of the kitchen

Fritz emerges in a blast of steam. He takes bread from his pocket and puts crumbs down for the mice

Thompson enters dressed as a porter and carrying a big crate of pots and pans

Thompson (*to Fritz*) Hello. Polish lads told me this is where you hide away. We've never said hello properly.

No reply

Bit of a loner, eh? German? Hear you joined the army early. Lied about your age. You must have been a brave kid.

No reply

Well, I'll leave you to it. Better get back or I'll be in trouble. Don't want them cancelling my half-day. I'm taking Alice, you know from housekeeping, up to Crosby again. You got a girl? Back home in Germany? Things are tough there I know. I met this guy from Berlin. He was saying … Well anyway. I'm Thompson. Just being friendly. (*He starts to go but returns*) Should you be doing that? I mean feeding vermin? I mean it's a kitchen after all.

Fritz They come anyway. Why pretend they don't. The mice are no harm. It's the rats you've got to watch for. There's a rat problem in Germany.

The music intro to No. 7 starts

Thompson Listen, you ever been to Crosby? It's very pretty. Maybe if you got out of here sometime, got a bit of sunlight, sea air.

Fritz isn't listening

No. 7 Rats

Fritz (*intensely*) Rats are very cunning.
They wait and watch your weakness as they cower.
And all the time they're breeding,
As their waiting, watching, feeding till the hour
When they're stronger than you, bigger than you
Then they pounce and gather up the shoots and seeds
Till everything and everyone the rat has touched
Becomes weak and diseased.

Thompson (*breezily*) Blundell ain't Bermuda but it's fun,
Try it, Fritzy,
Paddling in the sea when your work is done
Feeling frisky.
Keep your California I want Crosby's sun
With a candyfloss and bag of chips to come.
Get a little sand beneath your toes
That'll sort you.
What will tomorrow bring us?
No one knows
So why worry
Forget your troubles
Grab yourself a brolly and head
To the Wirral Riviera scene instead.

Fritz Mice are very diff'rent.
Mice won't overwhelm you, each adapts.
Though rats may rule the kingdom now,
Other forces plan ingenious traps.
And the kingdom of mice, will return to the mice,
Free from the old tyranny they face.

Act I, Scene 4   23

>Till that day I nourish them like one day,
>I'll inspire the human race.

The scene moves to the hotel reception area

>*Young Alice is bustling around Reception with her friend Babs, a chambermaid, blonde, brassy and blousy*

>*The music underscore continues throughout*

Babs Oh Alice, not another day out with that kitchen boy? How many times have I got to tell you? A good marriage is our ticket out of here and this New Year's Eve we get to flirt with the most powerful men in the world. Don't go throwing yourself away on a skivvy.
Young Alice He's not a skivvy. He's actually very brilliant. He's down in the kitchen at the moment because … well, he had something to prove to me. And he's shaping up really well.
Babs He's a looker, I'll give you that. If he's going up in the world too you'd better snap him up before someone else does.
Young Alice Do you think?
Babs Sounds to me like you'd better stake your claim, girl.

Back to the kitchen area

>*Young Alice and Babs exit*

Fritz	The rich are getting richer
	As they kick the honest German in the face.
Thompson	There's a bandstand.
Fritz	The great war brought us to our knees
	The traitors at Versailles betrayed our race.
Thompson	Punch and Judy
Fritz	But not any more, we'll even the score.
Thompson	Well nice to meet you,
	Toodle pip!
	We'll catch up again.
	You'll love Blundell Sands,
	There's an oom-pa-pa brass band
	Sunshine feels so grand.
	Auf Wiedersehen!

Fritz and Thompson exit

Young Alice enters the kitchen area

There is a commotion. Young Alice is harassed by Paddy and Henri

No. 7A Harassment underscore

Henri Wait a minute, pretty lady?
Paddy We don't get so many visitors down here, do we, Henri?
Henri Going to help scrub the pots, gorgeous?
Paddy Bet you're good at scrubbing. Got any Irish in you? Do you want some?
Henri Perhaps a friendly kiss, my sweet.

Henri grabs Young Alice for his kiss

Thompson enters

Thompson Get off. Leave her alone. She's mine. Get off my girl.

Underscoring out

Young Alice, perfectly in control, hits Henri on the jaw

Young Alice Get off, you greasy pig. Anyone else want to dance with this fist in their gob?

Paddy and Henri look sheepish

Fred, Fritz and other kitchen staff arrive

(*Turning to Thompson*) What did you just call, me?
Thompson What?
Young Alice Just then, what did you call me?
Thompson My girl?
Young Alice That's what I thought you said.
Fred Lucky blighter!
Henri Sorry, Thompson.
Paddy We wouldn't have messed with her if we'd known.
Young Alice (*to Paddy and Henri*) You don't treat any woman like that d'you understand or God help you if I get to hear about it.
Fritz Pleased to meet you *Fräulein* ——?

Act I, Scene 4   25

Young Alice Alice.
Fritz *Wilkommen* to hell "*verlobte*" of Thompson.
Thompson What on earth are you doing down here?
Young Alice What does "*verlobte*" mean?
Fritz It's German for fiancée.
Young Alice Oh? And was your mate interpreting the situation correctly?
Thompson If I asked you to marry me, you'd run a mile. Or you should do.
Young Alice Would I?
Thompson As a matter of fact, there is something I've been meaning to tell you. Ask you. But not here. Let's talk about it later at the seaside.
Young Alice (*overjoyed*) Oh Thompson, I knew it. (*Snapping out of it*). But ... but ... that's what I came to say. I can't make it this afternoon. The first of the Hollywood lot are arriving. Lord Rothmore wants everything perfect. But I'll meet you up on the roof at midnight and you can ask me then. And just to give you some idea of what the answer will be.

She grabs and kisses him full on the mouth

(*Playfully threatening him with her fist*) Now, get back to work or you'll be seeing stars of a different kind.

Young Alice leaves

Paddy (*approaching Thompson*) Well, aren't you full of surprises? And to think, we all had you down as a pansy.
Thompson That lovely lady is my ticket out of the dish water and up that white-tiled staircase to accounts. I can get some savings behind me. Then who knows where I'll end up.
Paddy She's going to find out sooner or later the kind of man you are.
Thompson Oh yeah? And what kind would that be?
Paddy The kinda guy no girl should fall in love with.

The Lights change from the kitchen area to the hotel entrance as the carpet is unrolled up to the entrance

No. 8 Red Carpet Rolldown

SCENE 5

A red-carpeted Adelphi entrance; 1930s. Adelphi roof; the present

Older Alice and Jo are on the roof. Babs is in the hotel entrance area

Older Alice   That was the New Year's Eve Hollywood came to the Adelphi *en route* to a glittering reception for the American film industry at Buckingham Palace.

Carlos Gardel walks down the red carpet flanked by suave Hollywood leading men and press photographers

My mate Babs took one look at Paramount studio's tango star Carlos Gardel and just knew he was husband material. The trouble was everybody else knew he was set to marry his latest co-star.
Babs   (*aside*) Not if I've got anything to do with it. (*She sings*)

No. 9 A Wedding and a Yacht

Babs is at the centre of a stylized "Diamonds-Are-A-Girl's-Best-Friend" fantasy routine with the Hollywood men. She sings

>Demand a first-class service
>I'm your chambermaid of choice
>Don't put up with less than what I've got.
>All you need to do for me's
>Slip me a small gratuity,
>Like … shall we say
>A wedding and a yacht.

>And if a yacht's too much I'll settle for a villa
>In the South of France, maybe an ocean view
>Baby, call reception I'll come running
>I got champagne chilling just for two.

>You deserve the finest
>So don't compromise tonight,
>Let me serve you nibbles with your drink.
>All you need to do for me's
>Slip me a small gratuity
>Like … shall we say
>A wedding and a mink.

Act I, Scene 5

> And if a mink's too much I'll settle for a sable
> Or damn it, really any kind of fur
> As long as I look good as your fiancée
> When I'm treading the red carpet 'stead of her.
> 'Stead of her.

(*Speaking*) Gentlemen of the press? (*Indicating Carlos Gardel*) Get a load of my very own MGM — "Mersey Girl's Millionaire."

The Photographers' flash bulbs pop around her as, in a stylized segue, Babs, draped over Carlos Gardel, acts up for the cameras

Men
> If rubies cost too much
> Then bring her diamonds
>
> If sapphires cost too much
> Then bring her pearl
>
> But don't blow money, brother, on a sports car.

Babs
> I'm a sweet old-fashioned
> Rolls-Royce kinda girl.
>
> I think you've got the message
> I'll just reiterate
> I hope you have a very pleasant stay,
> Whilst movie starlets let you down
> I'll never disappoint
> Your future bride is just a call away.

Vamp continues under the following

Lord Rothmore Welcome to the Adelphi Hotel, sir. I hope you'll enjoy the New Year's Eve party we've arranged for you and your Hollywood friends tonight.
Carlos Gardel Can't wait. Is my fiancée checked in yet?
Lord Rothmore Not yet, sir.
Carlos Gardel (*making eyes at Babs*) Then maybe I'll retire and order a little room service.
Lord Rothmore (*impervious*) Of course, sir.
Babs I'm ready for my close up! (*She sings*)

> All you need to do for me's
> Slip me a small gratuity

>   Like … shall we say
>   A wedding and a —
>   A full on fairy tale wedding and a —
>   A big fat Hollywood wedding and a —

(*Speaking*) Christ, just a wedding'll do!!

Bump

Scene 6

A swanky New Year's Eve party in the Adelphi ballroom. The past: that night

No. 10 Cocktail Party underscoring starts

Lord Rothmore and Young Alice, surrounded by waitresses with trays of champagne, survey the swanky Hollywood party

Lord Rothmore (*to Alice*) Doesn't the Adelphi look wonderful tonight, Miss Summers?

Young Alice It's like a fairy tale, your lordship.

Lord Rothmore It's the most glittering New Year's Eve party Britain has ever seen. It would seem there's nothing like Hollywood royalty to coax every hanger-on from Westminster to Widnes out of the woodwork. (*Pointing people out*) There's the leader of the opposition, the Littlewoods brothers, the Foreign Secretary.

Rose (*a waitress*) Who are the Russians, your lordship?

Lord Rothmore Oh, they're from the Moscow State Circus, they'll perform their daredevil act from our roof at midnight after the fireworks.

Fred, the bellboy, passes and overhears

And the cowboy is Mr Roy Rogers, he's to ride his famous horse right up to our front desk in front of the press. It'll be a sensation.

Fred I love his films.

Lord Rothmore I'm afraid I'm a little greyer on the rest of our new American friends. The lady in the fox fur for instance.

Maisie (*a waitress*) That's Myrna Loy, sir. Ooh I loved her in *Vanity Fair*.

Dorothy (*a waitress*) And that's Joan Blondell, star of *Public Enemy*.

Act I, Scene 6   29

Lilly (*a waitress*) Doesn't John Barrymore look a dream boat?
Lord Rothmore Now, now, Miss Greggson.
Lilly Sorry, sir.
Dorothy Frederick March said I had lovely eyes.
Lord Rothmore Did he indeed?
Rose (*a waitress*) Looks like he's using the same line on Gloria Stuart.
Young Alice Over there in the lilac dress isn't that … ?

Everyone looks and gasps

Lord Rothmore Ah yes, I believe so. Exquisite creature.
Young Alice Isn't she tiny? It's funny the way you expect the stars to be well … bigger.
Lord Rothmore They're just the same as you and I. The only difference between you and Miss Lilac is opportunity. But you seem very happy with your lot. I don't believe you've stopped smiling all night.
Young Alice I'm very happy, sir, happy to be here. Happy to be part of this and …
Lord Rothmore (*playfully*) Miss Summers, are you in love?
Young Alice Certainly not, sir, not on company time.
Lord Rothmore I'm very glad to hear it. (*Beat*) He's a very lucky man.

Her Ladyship enters followed by her daughter, Druscilla

Her Ladyship Edgar, we're very impressed. Very, very impressed. Aren't we, Druscilla?
Druscilla Very impressed, Mother.
Her Ladyship I want to write you a cheque for the remaining shares this instant. Druscilla! Where's my reticule? I had it a moment ago.
Druscilla Mother, why must you lose everything?
Lord Rothmore (*ushering Her Ladyship and Druscilla out*) I'm sure we can find it, when did you last see it, your ladyship? (*Behind Her Ladyship's back he turns and smiles at Young Alice*)

Her Ladyship and Druscilla exit

(*As he goes, to someone off*) Mr Goldberg how lovely to have you with us.

Lord Rothmore exits. The Waitresses disperse

Underscoring out. There is the sound of party background chatter

Babs approaches dressed as a cigarette seller with a tray of wares

Babs Cigarettes, get your cigarettes here, cigars, gum!
Young Alice Babs, what on earth are doing in that outfit?
Babs It's the only way I could get in here. Gloria lent me it. She's on a break.
Young Alice Well you've had a gawp, now get out of here before you get us both into trouble.
Babs Just give me five minutes. I'm on the hunt. And anyway I came to tell you it's two minutes to midnight. Aren't you meeting thingy on the roof?
Young Alice Don't you think I know that? I've had my eyes glued to my watch all night.
Babs Alice, I hope you get what you want ... I mean that he proposes and all. What you two have ... well it's the real thing, isn't it? Course it wouldn't suit me, I'm after a movie star but — hope it works out for you, kid.
Young Alice Thanks, Babs. I love him so much.
Babs Well, what are you standing there for? Get up there. I'll cover for you.
Young Alice I think I should make him wait a little, don't you?
Babs Oh, yeah, 'course.

Pause

Young Alice Right, I think he's waited long enough. I'll be on the roof.
Babs Good luck.

Young Alice exits

Babs has another go at being a cigarette girl

Cigarettes! Cigarettes! Chewing gum.

A Russian Acrobat approaches

First Russian Acrobat Pretty lady, my friends and I, we are circus people, we like to have drink, proper drink, not this Europe champagne, where is vodka?
Babs I'm sorry, sir. We've only instructions to serve champagne.
First Russian Acrobat (*surreptitiously offering her money*) But it is your New Year's Eve! Perhaps you have friend who can help? You look like party girl to me.

Act I, Scene 6   31

Babs You need to talk to a guy called Thompson, Comrade. He'll sort yah. He's on the roof right now.
First Russian Acrobat *Spasiba!*

The First Russian Acrobat goes

A drunken American guest passes

Babs Cigarettes, sir?
Drunk (*a very slow American drawl*) Why, looky here. Say, Missie, I don't mind if I do.

Carlos Gardel enters

Underscore for Carlos Gardel's entrance

Babs sees Carlos Gardel, wants to get to him, and becomes frustrated with the slowness of her customer dithering over his choice of cigarette brand

Now, shall I have some of these little babies or these puppies?
Babs (*elbowing the drunk out the way to get to Carlos Gardel*) Get 'em round the corner at Lime Street, mate, they're cheaper. (*She darts over to Carlos Gardel's side and becomes sexy*) Cigarettes? Chewing gum? Me?

Carlos Gardel looks at her

That last item was just a special offer for you, kidder, but I think you know that.
Carlos Gardel What are you doing here?
Babs Maybe I just can't get enough of you Mr Tango King of Hollywood. Wow, you were amazing earlier. I felt like Loretta Young in *Call of the Wild*.
Carlos Gardel Young lady, I'm afraid I've no idea what you're talking about.
Babs I get it. Our little secret for now. I suppose the world'll find out soon enough.
Carlos Gardel Listen to me, you little tramp ——

He is interrupted by Her Ladyship and Druscilla

Her Ladyship (*off, calling her lost dog*) Mr Woofles! Mr Woofles!

Her Ladyship crosses with Druscilla

Her Ladyship (*to Carlos*) Have you seen my darling little dog?
Carlos Gardel (*with a suave little bow*) Alas no, beautiful lady.
Her Ladyship (*as she leaves*) He must be around here somewhere.

Her Ladyship exits

Druscilla (*explaining to Carlos as she leaves*) She loses everything.

Druscilla exits

Carlos Gardel (*to Babs, once they're alone*) The world finds out nothing, you hear? I've dealt with whores like you in every hotel from Baltimore to Buenos Aries. You had your piece of ass, you got paid, now get lost or I'll have them throw you out even quicker than you got into my pants.
Babs But you said a girl like me's for keeps.
Carlos Gardel Don't make me complain to the management about your pitiful and deeply unwelcome harassments. Who do you think they'll believe? Me or some cheap trash like you? (*Hollywood smarm*) Enjoy your evening, Blondie.

There is a commotion off

Fritz (*off*) You must let me in. I demand to see the British Foreign Secretary.
Carlos Gardel What the hell's going on?

Carlos Gardel exits

Fritz bursts in, filthy from the kitchen

Fritz (*yelling at someone in the direction of the auditorium*) Foreign Secretary of England, you must accept the terrible consequence of your Treaty of Versailles on the starving people of my country.

Men rush on and try to restrain him

(*Struggling*) Admit that you are part of an international conspiracy to bring the German people to their knees!

The Men bundle Fritz out

Babs is left dejected and alone

Act I, Scene 6   33

Babs (*bawling her eyes out*) Cigarettes, chewing gum, me! Anybody!?

Hollywood's Roy Rogers, in a cowboy style version of evening dress, enters. He approaches Babs. He is attentive and kind with a Texas accent

Hollywood's Roy Rogers Say, don't cry, honey. Do you know that guy?
Babs No.
Hollywood's Roy Rogers You upset about them there Germans too?
Babs (*pulling herself together*) No. (*Bawling again*) I just want to meet a nice Hollywood millionaire who'll take care of me.
Hollywood's Roy Rogers Sweet Pea, would I do? I certainly been to Hollywood.
Babs (*brightening*) Well that's promising.
Hollywood's Roy Rogers Can't stick it though. Can't wait to get back to Rockville.
Babs (*bawling*) I want a rich one. (*Noticing the cowboy style fringing on his dinner jacket*) Look, your dinner jacket's all ragged.
Hollywood's Roy Rogers Honey, that's the fashion where I come from.
Babs Do they have swimming pools there and valet parking?
Hollywood's Roy Rogers Not so much I guess.

Babs wails

Oh little lady. There must be something about me you like. (*He sings cowboy style*)

No. 11 Yippee Ai Eh!

Can you picture us camping in the wilderness?
Singin' to my old guitar?
The snakes won't bother you, no ma'am
Wishing on a western star.
We could saddle up Trigger and Bessie
Our hearts as high as a hawk.
You'll fit right in at the hay and feed store
Say, try some Cowfolk talk.

"Yippee Ai eh!"
Means I'm happy
"Yippe Ai Oh"

                    But I'm lonesome.
                    "Come and git it"
                    Means I'm russlin' up
                    Some fine pork belly stew.
                    "Amigos" gettin' friendly
                    We could "Boot skoot"
                    That means dancin'
                    You're a "buckaroo piece of heaven"
                    Means I sure am stuck on you.

Babs   Mate, it's just like Liverpool,
                    We've got our expressions too.

                    "Come 'ed"
                    Means come nearer
                    "Shurrup"
                    Means shut up, mate
                    "Sof' lad"
                    Means you're crazy
                    And I'm not made up with you.
                    "You're doin' me 'ead in"
                    Means just sling it,
                    You're a scone 'ead
                    So forget it,
                    "Ta ra, Divvy"
                    Means goodbye, old son,
                    The language lesson's through.

Hollywood's Roy Rogers "Yippee Ai eh!"
Babs   Means you're happy. But "Shurrup" —
Hollywood's Roy Rogers Means that you ain't
                    But "Come and git it"
                    Means I'm russlin' up
                    Some pork and beans for you.
Babs   You're doin' me 'ead in
Hollywood's Roy Rogers Means hey whoa there
                    We could "Boot skoot"
Babs   We're not dancin'
Hollywood's Roy Rogers You're a "buckaroo piece of heaven"
Babs   How'd I get the message through.

(*Speaking to distract him*) Look there's a wigwam.

Act I, Scene 7   35

Hollywood's Roy Rogers looks

  Babs runs off

Hollywood's Roy Rogers (*in frustration, having lost her*) Darn it!

The music resolves

                           SCENE 7

On the Adelphi roof; the past

Thompson runs to joins Young Alice, who's been waiting by the edge of the parapet

Thompson (*seeing the drop and pulling himself up short*) Whoa! Too near the edge here!

They laugh

>   Sorry I'm late. It's crazy down there. That German guy — Fritz, he's in some sort of trouble. He's given the police the slip and they're looking everywhere for him. They say he's a spy.
> **Young Alice** I thought you weren't coming.
> **Thompson** Alice, you're the best thing that's ever happened to me.
> **Young Alice** Is that right?
> **Thompson** And I'm going to make you proud.
> **Young Alice** You'd better.
> **Thompson** Couldn't you get me a book-keeping job here and get me out of that kitchen?
> **Young Alice** (*playfully*) Isn't there something else you want to ask me first?
> **Thompson** (*kindly*) Oh Alice, you want me to ask you to marry me?
> **Young Alice** Yes.
> **Thompson** I can't marry you.
> **Young Alice** Why not?
> **Thompson** If I was to ever settle down with a girl I'd want it to be a girl like you.
> **Young Alice** If?
> **Thompson** Well, I'm not in any hurry. Are you? It just wouldn't work out … I'm … I'm just not … I let people down.
> **Young Alice** You don't love me?

Thompson No. Well, yes, yes very much. I do love you.
Young Alice Then what's the problem? Men! Cowards the lot of you.
Thompson I'm not a coward!
Young Alice Then what are you scared of?
Thompson It's not that I'm scared. It's just ... You're special, what we have ... I don't want things between us to go sour when you find out that in London ——
Young Alice When I find out you're a coward.

Fritz edges along a ledge below them. This can be elaborately staged or simply achieved by having Young Alice and Thompson standing confidently upstage of a barrier whilst, downstage of it, Fritz edges nervously along as if he's on a high ledge

Fritz (*calling up*) I went to Blundell Sands like you said. It was horrible.
Thompson (*to Fritz*) What are you doing up here?
Fritz I'm going to make a spectacular protest for the fatherland. I shall throw myself from the hotel at midnight and ruin their New Year celebrations.
Young Alice (*alarmed*) Thompson!
Thompson Right, I'll show you who's a coward. (*He climbs down towards Fritz*)
Young Alice Thompson!
Fritz What are you doing?
Thompson I'm rescuing you.
Fritz But I do not wish to be rescued.
Thompson (*looking down*) Jeeeeez!
Fritz What's the matter?
Thompson I'm terrified of heights.
Young Alice Well what did you climb down for then, you mug?

Fritz nimbly climbs to safety alongside Young Alice

Fritz Do not be frightened. Just reach up to me.
Thompson Can't. Can't move.
Young Alice Thompson, just don't look down, close your eyes take deep breaths.

Babs arrives

Babs Alice, what's going on?
Young Alice Thompson's stuck on the ledge.

Act I, Scene 7   37

Babs What's he doing on the ledge?
Young Alice Being an idiot.
Babs Well, I came to tell you, he needs to get back down to the kitchen. The police want to talk to him about that crazy German.
Fritz *Gutten Abend, Fräulein.*
Babs God, it's like Central Station up here.

Her Ladyship and Druscilla pass across the roof calling for their lost dog

Her Ladyship
Druscilla } (*together*) Mr Woofles! Mr Woofles! Mr Woofles!
Thompson (*ignoring them*) Excuse me, Babs isn't it?

Her Ladyship and Druscilla exit

Babs Yes.
Thompson I may possibly die within the next few moments. I want you to deliver a message to someone.
Babs What? Who?
Thompson That girl up there, that girl that wants to marry me. Tell her — (*He sings*)

No. 12 Tell Her

	Tell her she's wonderful.
Babs	He says you're wonderful
Thompson	And if she wants to take a chance on me
	I will do everything, and I mean everything
	To try to be all she needs me to be.
	If a man ever could
	Turn round his life for good
	I'll be that man, I'm giving her my word.
	You're right, I've been too cowardly
	Please Alice will you marry me?
	Could someone help me up?
Babs	He says —
Young Alice	(*speaking in time to the music*) *I heard.*
	I don't know what to say
	How'd things turn out this way?
Babs	She's me mate,
	You mess with her
	You're dead.

                 I s'pose he thinks he's smooth?
                 Well then he'd better prove
                 Why I shouldn't push him off that ledge.

Thompson (*yelling*) No!

  (*Singing*)   I'll promise anything!
Babs   A proper wedding ring?
Thompson   Yes the finest ring they have on show.
Young Alice (*suddenly alarmed*)
                You all right?
Babs   He looks a fright.
Thompson   And I don't want to die tonight.
Young Alice   He's going very green
Fritz   (*speaking in time to the music*) It's vertigo.

Thompson (*speaking*) Can't move. Going to fall.

The underscore for Trigger's entrance begins

    Hollywood's Roy Rogers suddenly appears in full rhinestone cowboy glory on a white horse. Or at least we see him pulling a taut rope from the wings that looks as if he's leading an off stage horse

Hollywood's Roy Rogers Want for me to lasso him?
Young Alice Oh my God! There's a horse! A horse on the roof of the Adelphi Hotel. Just a minute. Is that … Is that … Trigger?
Hollywood's Roy Rogers Sure is!
Young Alice Mr Rogers, you're both going to have to go back inside. The new year fireworks will start any minute and ... the roof is strictly out of bounds for … pets.
Hollywood's Roy Rogers Trigger's been around plenty of gun powder. It seems to me you need a cowboy and I got to prove to this young lady I'm worth taking a chance on. (*To Babs*) Would you have supper with me tomorrow?
Babs Look, mister ——
Young Alice (*pointedly*) Babs, this is Mr Roy Rogers. The millionaire cowboy star.
Babs Star? Millionaire?!
Young Alice That's right.
Babs (*very keen on Roy now*) Well yippee ai eh! Why didn't you say so, amigo.

Act I, Scene 7   39

Underscore out

   The six Russian Acrobats turn up

First Russian Acrobat (*to Babs*) Hey pretty lady, we start show any minute after fireworks. Where is your friend with drink?
Thompson Excuse me, man clinging to ledge here!
Second Russian Acrobat Where is "knock off" vodka?
Thompson In the water tank!
Young Alice (*horrified*) Thompson!

   The Acrobats go to check it out

Fritz (*tearfully*) Such a beautiful horse, like in Austria where I grew up.
Hollywood's Roy Rodgers (*to Fritz*) You going to help me rescue this guy, compadre?
Fritz Why not. I make my protest tomorrow. Liverpool not so bad.

   During the following, they coax Thompson up on to the roof

Babs Alice, he's a real life Hollywood star. And he wants me —
Young Alice Nothing ever goes like you expect up here.
Babs What you going to do about Thompson?

   The intro to Act I Finale starts

Young Alice Well, if he can get me a ring like he promised at least I'll know he's serious.
Babs He's a kitchen porter, Alice, how's he going to afford a ring?
Young Alice I don't know. But it's New Year's Eve and I'm on a hotel roof with a German spy, a movie star, six Russian acrobats and a horse! This is the Adelphi — anything can happen!

No. 13 Act I Finale

Babs (*singing*)	The stars are calling out our name
Young Alice	It's Liverpool's time again
Babs } **Young Alice**	At last my heart is waking.
Young Alice	Shout the news across the sky
Babs } **Ensemble**	Ah … Ah … Ah …

Tonight it's you and I
Who'll choose the road we're taking.

Thompson has reached safety by now and is being comforted by Fritz and Hollywood's Roy Rodgers

As everyone sings, Thompson slowly pulls himself to his feet to face Young Alice

All For tonight
If we dream
The world will dream along with us
We waited long enough, now is the right time

The six Russian Acrobats return with bottles of vodka

If we fail then we fail but at least we chose to fight

They hand bottles to everyone

Don't waste tonight's
Once in a lifetime.

Russian Acrobats (*speaking, raising bottles to the front*) Na zdorovje!
Everyone else (*speaking, raising bottles to the front*) Happy New Year!

During the following, Her Ladyship and Druscilla return dejected having failed to find Mr Woofles but at the last moment Lord Rothmore arrives and hands them the lost dog

Everyone faces out front except Thompson and Young Alice who face each other

Older Alice returns to watch

All Don't waste tonight's
Once in a lifetime!

Choir Once in a lifetime!

New Year fireworks explode

END OF ACT I

ACT II

No. 14 Entr'acte

SCENE 1

The roof of the Adelphi Hotel; the present. The Accounts Department; the past

There is the sound of wind

Neil joins Jo

Neil Your nutter hasn't jumped, has he?
Jo No, and Miss Summers isn't a nutter, she's great. Listen, you want to hear her stories.
Neil No. I don't. I want to hear that you'll leave for Japan with me tomorrow.
Jo Oh Neil, I don't know. I'm really tempted but I haven't had a chance to think, it's a big decision.
Neil Then come and check out the websites with me and let the old loony jump if she wants to.
Jo That's a horrible thing to say.
Neil Where is she anyway?
Jo (*not concerned*) I don't know. Your ugly mug probably scared her off.
Neil Jo, there's nobody up here.
Jo Well, she's around somewhere. Just chill out, will you? I'm enjoying her memories. She worked here when all the Hollywood stars stayed in the old days.
Neil But that would make her a million years old. She's just some dotty old dear who's all confused.
Jo She's not. Well, except she's expecting to meet her boyfriend up here. Look I'll be down soon. Just give me a minute to make sure she's all right.
Neil Be careful. Her name's Summers, right?
Jo Yes, Alice Summers.
Neil Should I call the police?
Jo No! Don't you dare. I can handle it.

Neil Hope you're right.

Neil goes

No. 14A "Alice Reappears" underscoring starts

Older Alice enters

Older Alice My dear, you're still here. No need to wait with me if you've better things to do. I'll be quite all right on my own.
Jo No, that's OK. I don't want you to be alone. Anyway I want to hear more about the old days. What happened to that German, Fritz?
Older Alice Fritz, he was deported I think. Anyway we thought we'd heard the last of him.
Jo And that was how the story started that Hitler worked here?
Older Alice Exactly, all a load of rubbish.
Jo And the cowboy and his horse staying here?
Older Alice No that really happened, it was the sight of that horse up here in the moonlight that convinced me to think Thompson was right. This roof is a very special place.
Jo Did he give you a wedding ring?
Older Alice Well ... yes ... and no.
Jo The two of you didn't have much spare cash I guess.
Older Alice Things weren't so tight after I got him his beloved job in accounts. Well, I couldn't marry a kitchen porter now, could I? You should have seen him, back in a suit, like the cat who got the cream, all dapper and turning heads. The secretaries couldn't take their eyes off him.

The intro starts. Jo becomes Young Alice

No. 15 Thompson from Accounts

Tap dancing Secretaries and Accountants appear for this fantasy Busby Berkeley routine

Girls   He's got dash with cash,
                   He's a beaut with loot,
                   He got style in large amounts
                   He's an adding machine Adonis
                   He's Thompson from accounts.

Thompson enters the routine

Act II, Scene 1   43

Thompson   Things are adding up for Thompson
                 Didn't amount to much before but, see.
                 Now, on balance I'm in profit
                 Hey world better take account of me.
                 Honey, let's forget our long division
                 From now on I'll times everything by two.
                 There's no point subtracting,
                 It's me that you're attracting,
                 I'm hoping I can come to count on you?

Girls   Over in wages
                 It's outrageous
                 Everything's awry.
                 No one's getting paid this week,
                 Paperwork sky high.
                 Never fear
                 Salvation's here.
                 Banish all your doubts.
                 He's hunky, hot and heavenly,
                 He's Thompson from accounts.

Boys   Our supplier's
                 Getting tired
                 Bills have not been paid.
                 Invoices have been ignored
                 That's no way to trade.
                 But that's changing,
                 Re-arranging,
                 Everybody shouts
                 "Let's hear it for the legendary
                 Thompson from accounts."

All   Thompson ah ah ah ah ah,
                 Thompson ah ah ah ah ah
                 Always aims to please.
                 Thompson ah ah ah ah,
                 Thomp-ah-son ah ah ah ah,
                 The double entry, petty cash,
                 Accountant Hercules.

Older Alice Things were adding up for Thompson
                 Everybody loved him as you see.
                 He helped Adelphi finances to profit,
                 Insisting his success was thanks to me.

Thompson (*to Jo as Young Alice*)
    Honey, let's forget our long division,
    From now on I'll times everything by two.
    There's no point subtracting,
    It's me that you're attracting,
    I'm hoping I can come to count on you?

Older Alice (*speaking*) I was the envy of every woman he met. If only they knew.

A blast of "Rule Britannia" heralding the arrival of Britannia herself

Britannia enters and sings

Britannia Britannia used to rule the waves,
    But things are looking bleak.
    My subjects are deserting me
    It worsens by the week.
    Is there no young Argonaut
    To turn my fate about?
    Yes, look! Ahoy!
    I love that boy!
    It's Thompson from accounts.

Britannia exits

Girls   He's got dash with cash,
    He's a beaut with loot,
    He got style in large amounts.
    Accountancy's Adonis
    He's Thompson from accounts.

Vamp under the following

Someone from the Crowd (*speaking*) When are you two going to name the day then?
Thompson We're saving up. I want to do things properly. Like in a fairytale.
Young Alice Shouldn't be too long now ——

All   Things are adding up for Thompson,
    Didn't amount to much before but, see.
    Now, on balance he's in profit.

Act II, Scene 2

Thompson Hey world better take account of me.

All Time you both forgot your long division,
From now on he'll times everything by two.
There's no point subtracting,
It's Thompson you're attracting.
Here's hoping, here's hoping, here's hoping.
He can come to count on you.

Thompson's an accountant and accountable to you!

Scene 2

Adelphi Hotel reception; the past

There are sound effects of a hotel reception

Thompson bumps into Babs

Babs What you looking so pleased with yourself about?
Thompson Should I conclude from your frosty demeanour that there's still no letter from the cowboy?
Babs Worse than that. Look.

She shows him a Hollywood magazine

Thompson (*reading*) "Cowboy heart throb Roy Rodgers to marry his childhood sweetheart." Oh Babs I'm sorry.
Babs Don't be. I never really liked him anyway, that bleedin' horse used to keep giving me funny looks. (*Referring to the couple's magazine picture*) Look at her. She was probably born with a saddle stuck to her arse.
Thompson Well I'm glad you're feeling so resilient.
Babs Men!

And Babs stomps off

A well-spoken, though shifty looking young man, Frank, approaches Thompson

Frank Still breaking hearts, then?
Thompson Frank? What are you doing here?

Frank Hitch-hiked up from London. Aren't you pleased to see me?
Thompson I thought you said you hated me.
Frank Oh I do. That's why I've come. Making a nice life for yourself here from the looks of things. Wish I could say the same.
Thompson Still not settled to anything?
Frank I haven't got any money, Thompson, my father cut me off without a penny, remember. I'm grubbing around living off bread and bacon in a crummy bedsit in Earls Court. Cockroaches live better then me. Can you imagine how that makes me feel? What I'm brooding on every night.
Thompson Me?
Frank You, Thompson, and how listening to you wrecked my life.
Thompson I never meant for things to turn out the way they did.
Frank No, how could you? You never think anything through. It's just about grabbing the moment, isn't it, and to hell with the consequences.
Thompson Actually I've changed.
Frank I've heard. Been asking around. So there's a girl in the picture now. I wonder how she'd feel if she knew about your spell in prison.
Thompson She knows I went a bit wild in the past. She wants me to move on.
Frank Well, isn't that nice. I wish my family could be more forgiving.
Thompson Lots of people get sent down from university.
Frank We were arrested for robbery, My father was a high court judge. His career was ruined. I don't think he'll find it as easy to shrug the matter off as your Scouse scrubber, do you?
Thompson When are you going to grow up and take some responsibility? It was your cousin, remember, you told me where the safe was.
Frank I was impressionable, naïve, little more than a child. You manipulated me just as surely as you ensnared all the women you wanted to bed. You were a Liverpool street rat. You took advantage. Well now it's my turn. You've got your new start. Now you're going to pay for mine. I've been to meetings in London, meetings about the civil war in Spain. I want to go there, lots of our kind are heading over, join the resistance, see if I can't find the backbone you crushed. But I'll need money. And you're going to give it to me.
Thompson I haven't got any money.
Frank You've got more than me. Look at that suit. See me in a suit, Thompson? And you're going to find me a lot more or I'll make sure your fiancée understands exactly the man you are.
Thompson Maybe it'd be for the best. I've been thinking about telling her anyway. Maybe she'll understand. Maybe she'll —

Act II, Scene 2   47

Frank I wouldn't count on it. And even if she does, Lord Rothmore's a family friend. I tip him off and you can wave goodbye to your nice hotel job and any other job round here I imagine. Maybe the future Mrs T won't be quite so understanding when you're both on the streets. Get me some money, Thompson, and me and this whole nasty business will go away.
Thompson How much do you want?
Frank My ticket over there plus enough cash to splash around and buy me some friends. I'll leave the amount up to you but you'd better make it enough to keep me sweet. And, as you know, I'm very bitter indeed.

Frank and Thompson exit. Babs enters

The Lights change and come up on Babs checking her make-up in a compact mirror. She sings

No. 16 Tell Them

Babs   Tell them
                    I'm very loyal
                    That I'm dependable.
                    Tell them Yanks I'd keep a lovely house.
                    They buy me little treats,
                    Chase me between the sheets
                    But no one takes me home to cook 'em scouse.
                    They say I've lovely eyes,
                    As they caress my thighs,
                    They pinch me bum
                    And call me "hun". All right,
                    If every kiss is perfect bliss
                    Then why'd I feel as bad as this?
                    And why'd they only want me for the night?

Thompson enters another area

Babs and Thompson are lit in their separate despair. Thompson sings

Thompson	I thought my past was done.
Babs	Thought I'd charm everyone.
Babs ⎫	
Thompson ⎭	But now the tide has turned, the water's deep.
	I used to think I owned the earth

> But now I see my real worth
> A shop-soiled former winner
> Going cheap.

Segue into No. 17 Bedroom underscore

Scene 3

A bedroom at the Adelphi Hotel; the past

Thompson is in the hotel bedroom of Hollywood's imposingly handsome and carnivorously sexual, Delores Gilmore. A sexually charged atmosphere

Delores Gilmore So I guess you're a fan, kid.
Thompson Yep, I never miss a Delores Gilmore movie. I hope this room's to your satisfaction. I couldn't believe it when I saw you in the lobby yesterday.
Delores Gilmore Yeah, I noticed you looking, kid. Like you were eating me up with those hungry eyes.
Thompson I'm sorry, Miss Gilmore.
Delores Gilmore No, don't apologize. That look you gave me was the reason I booked into this dump. Then wasn't that you skulking, just down the corridor last night? Were you hoping I might autograph something? Personal. I hate to disappoint a fan. So tell me about you.
Thompson Not much to tell really, I work in accounts here, live just —
Delores Gilmore Say kid, how about we cut a few corners. I'm guessing you're a good dancer, right?
Thompson I like to dance.
Delores Gilmore Yeah, I can tell by the way you slid into the lift right in front of me, just brushing my sleeve, reaching across me to press the button. "Dexterous" I believe is the word. So you going to do a little dance for me now?
Thompson What kind of a dance do you think you can afford, Miss Gilmore.
Delores Gilmore *(enjoying the game, tantalizing Thompson with a big wad of cash)* Like that, is it. Don't seem so desperate, kid. It's not a good look on you!
Thompson I'm sorry. I'm being blackmailed.
Delores Gilmore Thought I recognized the twitch. Bleeding you dry, right?
Thompson I've no savings. Nothing to sell — well, turns out nothing of value.

Act II, Scene 3											49

Delores Gilmore Oh I wouldn't say that. Shall we start with ten dollars? Don't know what that is in your money but it ought to buy me something, right? (*She sings*)

No. 18 Dance For Me, Boy

Dance for me, boy.
You know you want to.
Dance for me, boy
You know you've got to
Duck and dive and
Weave and slide
If you want to catch my eye
Come on and dance for me, boy!

Seen it all before
So many slim-hipped Joes like you —
Swagger and muscle.
Just another dope
Without a hope a-getting off skid row,
You've got to learn to hustle.
Look at you there,
You got potential.
You could be here
With just a gentle
Soft shoe shuffle routine,
Know what I mean?
Come on and dance for me, boy.

Dance for me, boy.
You know you want to.
Dance for me, boy
You know you got to
Duck and dive and
Weave and slide
If you want to catch my eye
Come on and dance for me, boy.

Kid you're kinda sweet
So let me give yah some advice.
Quit this one horse city.
You're hot, you got a chance
If you can dance your way to pastures new

> While you're young and pretty.
> So do me a show —

Thompson dances alluringly for her as she sings

> Go, let me pay for
> Your ticket out,
> I'm what you prayed for
> A rich and generous bitch,
> Who's got an itch,
> Snake those hips for me, boy.

(*Speaking*) Oh yeah, kid. You got what it takes. (*She sings*)

> Dance for me, boy.
> You know you want to
> Dance for me, boy
> You know you got to
> Duck and dive and
> Weave and slide
> If you want to catch my eye
> Come on and dance for me ——

They end up with their faces almost touching in a kiss. Thompson pulls away

Thompson No, this isn't who I am anymore. A year ago maybe.

Thompson starts to rush out

Delores Gilmore Say, where you going?
Thompson I'm sorry if I took advantage — I'm with someone now. It's all different.

Thompson exits

Delores Gilmore Lucky someone.

The music resolves. The Lights change

No. 18A Transition to Scene 4 starts

Scene 4

Adelphi Hotel reception; the past

Her Ladyship, with Druscilla in tow, is harassing bell boy, Fred

Her Ladyship Where the devil is my engagement ring? What is the matter with everyone in this ghastly place? Has the damp gone to your brain or something?

Jo as Young Alice approaches

Young Alice Thank you, Fred, I'll take care of this.
Fred (*aside*) Thanks, Miss S. Good luck.

The music finishes

   Fred leaves, gratefully

Young Alice I'm sorry, your ladyship, I wasn't able to find your ring in the lounge.
Her Ladyship It's been stolen. I told you, there's been a shifty young man, a young man in a sky blue tie hanging around me all day. Most suspicious. You must have seen him.
Young Alice I'm sorry, I haven't. And I think I would have noticed — my boyfriend wears a sky blue tie. With your permission we'll search your room.
Her Ladyship Yes, yes but I tell you, if it doesn't turn up soon I'm calling the police.

   Her Ladyship exits with Druscilla

Lord Rothmore approaches Young Alice

Lord Rothmore Miss Summers, may I have a word with you?
Young Alice Lord Rothmore. I was just on my way up to ——
Lord Rothmore Perhaps you're on your break.
Young Alice Well yes, I was just … I'm meeting … is there a problem, your lordship?
Lord Rothmore A problem … good heavens no. Quite the reverse, in fact … look, this won't take long, I've just come from a meeting of our directors. Perhaps you've heard Mr Pritchard is retiring.

Young Alice The place won't be the same without him.
Lord Rothmore Well no ... I suppose not. It does mean of course that we'll be looking for a new manager to work alongside Mr Noble and Mr Ryder. I've told the board that I cannot imagine anyone more suited to the task than you.
Young Alice Me ... but. Oh your lordship, me?
Lord Rothmore Yes, why not? A trifle unusual perhaps a female manager but why not? In America I gather ... well anyway, you deserve it. Your diligence and attention to detail, your cool head in a crisis, soothing manner with our American guests ... all in all ... Yes I think you'll make an excellent manager — manageress.
Young Alice I don't know what to say. Thank you.
Lord Rothmore Well just say yes, or well perhaps not now. Why don't you mull it over. Give me your decision in the morning.
Young Alice I can tell you what my answer will be right now, sir.
Lord Rothmore There is one other thing to bear in mind, the board think... As you know it's a demanding job... long hours. The board don't feel the job would suit ... well, a married lady. I'm sure you understand. The hotel must come first.
Young Alice (*shocked*) Yes ... yes I see that.
Lord Rothmore I hope I haven't dampened your enthusiasm.
Young Alice No ... no ... it's just ... well it's a lot to think about.
Lord Rothmore Yes, yes of course. Well, you mull it over. Let me know in the morning. (*Affectionately*) If I know you you'll go up to that blasted roof of yours, think it all through and come up with the right answer.
Young Alice I'll try, sir. Thank you.

Lord Rothmore leaves

Young Alice turns to face Thompson

SCENE 5

Thompson and Young Alice on the Adelphi roof; the past

Thompson Ladybird, Ladybird. I was hoping I'd find you here. Ladybird. Alice. (*Pause. He kneels*) Will you marry me?

Beat. She looks at him

Young Alice Oh, Thompson. Are you sure?

Act II, Scene 5   53

Thompson As sure as I've been of anything in my whole life. Meet me up here, same time next year, and every year for the next hundred years, and I'll tell you the same thing.
Young Alice Sound like you've got yourself a date, but I want champagne every anniversary, please, and dancing and — none of your nonsense.
Thompson Then you'll marry me?
Young Alice Of course I will. There's no job I'd choose over you, nothing I wouldn't give up to be with you. We can beat the world. Get through anything.
Thompson Really?
Young Alice Really.
Thompson Even if … I've just come from Ma, told her everything. She says I owe it to you to give you the whole picture, about my past I mean.
Young Alice (*misunderstanding*) No, Thompson, you don't. What's done is done. I want you for the man you are, the man you're going to be. Forget about the past.
Thompson (*remembering*) Well, we've got a ring now at least. (*He produces an engagement ring*)
Young Alice (*gasping with pleasure*) Oh Thompson! How did you afford this?
Thompson Well, I didn't exactly buy it. No money changed hands — put it that way.
Young Alice Well how … ? You didn't buy it? Where did you get it from? It looks familiar.
Thompson I suppose you could say we're borrowing it.
Young Alice Borrowing it?
Thompson Maybe one day our daughter will wear it. Maybe even a granddaughter — think of that.
Young Alice You're joking.
Thompson What's the matter?
Young Alice It was you, wasn't it? In the sky blue tie? Her Ladyship says she saw you watching her yesterday.
Thompson What? Oh Alice. All right, this is what we've got to talk about. There are things about me. Things about my past with women. Ghosts that won't go away. But I know now I can change. I want to. I lost the money I saved to buy you a ring. I was blackmailed.
Young Alice Blackmailed!
Thompson I wasn't thinking straight. The shock — My past catching up with me like that. I saw a bunch of rich women in the bar and I thought: what the hell, I'll make some money … the old way. One final time. For you.

Young Alice The old way?
Thompson It was wrong of me. A big, big mistake. I know that now. I don't deserve you, Alice, I was all set to pack my bags and run but Ma persuaded me to give it one more shot. Yes, it's her ring, but it was her ma's before that ... and she wants us to have it now.

Thompson notices the look of horror on her face

I thought you'd be pleased.
Young Alice A stolen engagement ring! You thought I'd be pleased with a stolen engagement ring? Don't you know me at all?
Thompson What? It's not stolen! You think I'd ... You honestly think I'd ...
Young Alice You'll say anything, won't you!? You'll even lie about your own mother! How stupid do you think I am? Her ladyship reported a missing ring last night.
Thompson (*flabbergasted*) Christ! You think ...
Young Alice Well you've done worse. Plenty. Look, just get lost will you. Before I push you off this goddamn roof. You lying cheating, scumbag.
Thompson Jeez, how could I have been so naïve? When you look at me a part of you always sees the thief you hid on this roof two years ago. (*Beat. Sadly*) There's no escaping the past is there, Alice?
Young Alice I wish to God I never met you.
Thompson Well, you're no fool, Ladybird.

Thompson leaves

Young Alice (*calling after him*) And don't come back! You make me sick!!!!! (*She sings*)

No. 19 The Next Ten Seconds

Get out of here
There's nothing left of me.
You've had the lot,
You've bled me dry
Now leave.

Try, go on fly your scene of crime,
I'll be ancient history in just ten seconds' time.
What happened to the girl I used to be?
Independent, confident and free.

Act II, Scene 6

> Wait! You can be that way again
> Close your eyes, don't think of him for one whole count of ten.
>
> Somehow, there's got to be a way to breathe.
> And come tomorrow I believe, I'll have a thought
> That you're not running through.
> I'm fine — Hey look and see how fine I am,
> I'm happy, I don't give a damn,
> 'Cos there's more to me than you.
>
> If I should call you back just turn and run.
> I'm battered and I'm bruised with all you've done.
> Soon I'll be strong and over you,
> It's just the next ten seconds,
> It's just the next ten seconds,
> It's just the next ten seconds;
> That may break my heart in two.
>
> It's just the next ten seconds;
> That may break my heart in two.

The Lights go down on Young Alice

No. 19A "Neil's Next Ten Seconds" begins

Scene 6

The Adelphi reception; the past (and briefly the present). Mo's house; the past

The Lights come up on Young Alice, Babs, Lilly and Rose in Reception

Babs You look terrible, kid.
Lilly Not surprised though. Bet you didn't sleep a wink.
Young Alice What do you mean?
Babs Must have been one hell of a row — Thompson giving in his notice and all.
Young Alice He what?
Babs Didn't you know?
Rose Took off before dawn this morning.
Young Alice Did he say where he was going?
Rose Just said things were getting too hot for him around here.

Lilly Don't you know where he's heading?
Young Alice No and I don't want to.

Young Alice exits

Babs Alice — (*But she realizes it's hopeless*)

Babs exits the other way with Lilly and Rose

Neil enters reception. He's talking on his mobile phone in today's Adelphi

Neil Hey mate, it's me. Look can't chat I'm at work and they're watching me like a hawk. Could you do me a favour? Could you do an internet search on "Alice Summers Adelphi Hotel"? Yep. Summers. Call me back if you find anything. (*He sings*)

No. 19A Neil's Next Ten Seconds

> Somehow I never got around to say,
> You brighten up the dullest day
> And when you're not around, my thoughts are filled with you.
> Why did I leave it up till now to say
> I loved you in a quiet way
> Just wish I'd told you too.

Neil exits

The Adelphi Hotel Reception back then

Young Alice bustles over to meet Her Ladyship

Young Alice Good morning, your ladyship. I hope you slept well.
Her Ladyship How was I supposed to sleep in this viper's nest of thievery.
Young Alice On behalf of everyone here at the Adelphi Hotel may I offer sincerest apologies for the theft of your engagement ring. (*Handing over the ring*) Your engagement ring I believe.

Her Ladyship takes the ring and stares at it

> We'd like you to know that we take our role as custodian of our guests' possessions very seriously and theft is extremely rare. We pride ourselves on dealing with the matter quickly and efficiently.

Her Ladyship Have you lost your reason, girl? (*Pointing at the ring*) What is that?
Young Alice I — I ... believe it's a diamond.
Her Ladyship A diamond? That little piece of glass? (*Handing Young Alice the ring*) Get this mockery away from me. I've never been so insulted in my life!
Young Alice This isn't your ring?

The intro to 19B "Young Alice's Next Ten Seconds (Reprise)" starts

Her Ladyship (*reading an inscription on the ring*) Certainly not. Read the inscription. Do I look like my name's "Annie-May"?
Young Alice But that's Thompson's nan! (*She sings*)

No. 19B Young Alice's Next Ten Seconds (Reprise)

>Soon I'll be strong and over you
>It's just the next ten seconds
>That may break my heart in two.

The tune segues into underscoring

Mo enters her home area

The Lights crossfade to Mo's house

Young Alice is talking to Mo, Thompson's mother

Mo Yes, it's my mam's ring, love. I'm afraid I don't know where they went. I don't think they knew themselves. Something about Spain, helping the wounded.
Young Alice The Spanish civil war. He's been reading about it in the papers.
Mo Listen, love, I'm not going to interfere, but you look just as unhappy as he did. Whatever it is you've quarrelled about, you'll patch things up. He left you a letter ——

Underscore out

Mo hands over the letter and exits

Young Alice opens it and begins to read

Thompson appears in a spotlight and voices what Young Alice is reading in the letter

Thompson Ladybird,
If you're reading this it means you've been to see Mam and probably know you misjudged me about that ring. I would never have started our life together like that. So you were wrong about that ... but you weren't wrong about me. That's why I'm leaving this morning. With me out of the picture maybe you'll find the type of kind, honourable man you deserve.

But please spare me a thought from time to time and don't let 'em work you too hard. (*He sings*)

No. 20 Take a Moment

Remember me some summer night in Liverpool
When every star above the dock's a precious jewel
When moonlight on the Mersey
Sends it silver to the sea — watch for a while, and think of me.
And in the chill of autumn, when the trees are bare
In Sefton Park remember me, and I'll be there.
No matter where tomorrow takes me, carried on its tide
Think of me from time to time, and I'll be at your side.

Grab a smile, they were meant for you and me
Fill your heart up to the brim
It's true the best things in life are free.
Yell if you can — laugh when you get a chance
Sing out that tune in your head
And always be the first one up to dance.

Remember me when spring breaks out on Merseyside
When every kid on Hope Street longs to play outside
And if you're still angry at the stupid things I've done
Remember how we had such fun!
Snowballing in Faulkner Square, our noses blue
Strolling out along the front at Waterloo
Cheering to the heavens when we score the winning goal
This city beats inside of me, I love it heart and soul.

Thompson Grab a smile, they were meant for you and me,
Young Alice Fill your heart up to the brim
It's true the best things in life are free.
Yell if you can — laugh when you get a chance

Act II, Scene 6

	Sing out that tune in your head
	And always be the first one up to dance.
Thompson	Sing out that tune
Young Alice	Sing out that tune,
Thompson	Sing out that tune in your head
Young Alice	And always be the first one up to dance!

The Lights change to the Adelphi Hotel reception

Thompson exits

Lord Rothmore is addressing the staff which includes Babs and Dorothy

Lord Rothmore And so tonight it is my happy duty to announce a historic appointment, the new assistant manager of the Adelphi Hotel will be a gal. I mean a woman ... I mean our very own Miss Alice Summers.

Young Alice looks ashen after the Thompson business

Staff Speech!
Young Alice I ... I ...
Babs Go on, kid. This is for all of us.
Young Alice Well this a great honour ... of course I ... I'm just not sure I ... I don't know if I ... there's just a knot inside me here.
Babs Yeah a big Thompson shaped knot!
Dorothy Alice, we all know you're hurting but you've been a good friend to everyone here. Seen us all through some tough times, we'll look after you.
Babs Say yes for us, for you. Don't say no for him.
Lord Rothmore Well, Miss Summers your decision please —

No. 21 Just Fine

Young Alice (*singing*)   Full English for a thousand
Ought to soothe a broken heart.
Nothing will replace him
But four hundred beds'll start.
If you think I can do it, sir
I'll make the old place shine
Everything is
Gonna be just fine.

Time passes and Older Alice takes over the song. From now on Alice is represented as Older Alice

   Young Alice exits

Older Alice   The 1930s went so fast
A whirl of highs and lows
A million daily crises
Means your confidence soon grows.
I steered this stately liner,
The guests poured through the door
Then suddenly we found ourselves at war.

   (*Slow, sad*)   Lord Rothmore went to Westminster
When Winston Churchill called
The news we heard from Europe
Left us frightened and appalled.
The rationing means things are tough
Our men have gone to fight
But chin up, girls

The rhythm picks up

   We're gonna be all right.

Babs   Alice, look, the American soldiers are on the dance floor again.

Scene 7

The ballroom of the Adelphi; the past

There is a microphone on a little stage

No. 22 Dance For Me, Boy (Reprise)

The men in American G.I. uniforms pile on and infectiously jitterbug with the girls led by Babs

G.I.s   Do Wah! Do Wah! Do Wah! Do Wah!
Do Wah! Do Wah! Do Wah! Do Wah!

The Girls, in an Andrews Sisters arrangement, sing

Act II, Scene 7

Babs and Girls	Do Wah! Do Wah! Do Wah! Do Wah! Do Wah! Do Wah! Do Wah! Do Wah! Dance for me, boy. You know you want to Dance for me, boy You know you got to Duck and dive and Weave and slide If you wanna catch my eye Come on and dance for me, boy!
All	You can't beat a boogie woogie dance tune
Ensemble	Ba-da-da, ba-da-da. Baah!
All	The latest jumping, jiving craze.
Ensemble	It's the latest jiving craze.
All	Glen Miller takes the stand, your spirits soar He'll banish all your blues away. And soon you're buzzing with the new tune
Ensemble	Ba-da-da, ba-da-da. Baah!
All	Those trumpets blowing something mean.
Ensemble	They'll be blowin' somethin' mean.
All	There's nothing sweller To a G.I. fella Than a full blown Boogie woogie dance routine.

Dance break and repeat as required. Then G.I. Brad Finkle and Babs sing a lead vocal

Brad and Babs	You can't beat a boogie woogie dance tune
Ensemble	Ba-da-da, ba-da-da. Baah!
Brad and Babs	The latest jumping, jiving craze.
Ensemble	It's the latest jiving craze.
Brad and Babs	Glen Miller takes the stand your spirits soar He'll banish all your blues away.
Ensemble	Ba ba ba ba, ba ba ba ba, ba ba, ba
Brad and Babs	And soon you're buzzing with the new tune
Ensemble	Ba-da-da, ba-da-da. Baah!
Brad and Babs	Those trumpets blowing something mean.
Ensemble	They'll be blowin' somethin' mean.
All	There's nothing sweller To a G.I. fella

Than a full blown
Boogie woogie dance routine.

Lilly approaches Older Alice during the applause

Lilly Alice, there's an overseas phone call for you in the front office.
Older Alice Thanks, Lil.

The dance fades away as Older Alice picks up the phone

Scene 8

Telephones at the Adelphi Hotel and in Germany

In Germany, Older Thompson, in an overcoat, is ringing Older Alice at the Adelphi Hotel

Older Alice Alice Summers speaking. (*Beat*) Who is this? (*Beat*) Is there anybody there?
Older Thompson Ladybird. You know what next month is, don't you? Alice … listen, I could lose this line at any moment. A long time ago I made you a promise, to meet you every year on the roof of the Adelphi Hotel and celebrate our love with a dance in the moonlight. Well it's been a few years since I made good on that promise, but I'm calling to say that next month nothing, nothing, will keep me away.
Older Alice Thompson!
Older Thompson I've fought for freedom all over Europe, seen some terrible things, done some terrible things and sometimes the only thing that reminds me I'm a human being is remembering what we once had and that's about the only thing I've never fought for, so Alice, I'll be up on that roof next month. Maybe you won't turn up, maybe you're married now, maybe you still hate me, but … well … I'll be there no matter what, just in case … just … in case you'd care to join me.
Older Alice Where are you?
Older Thompson On my way home, that's all you need to know. I've been working undercover in Europe.
Older Alice (*alarmed*) Thompson!
Older Thompson Funny thing, Ladybird, the mind of a thief's a valuable thing in war time.
Older Alice How did you ——
Older Thompson Let's say I had a little bit of help from the other side. Remember our German friend from the kitchens — he works for the resistance now, looks like we were a good influence.

Act II, Scene 9   63

> *Fritz, similarly overcoated, calls from the shadows*

Fritz Thompson, we have to get out of here. Now.
Older Thompson I'm coming home, Alice. I'm coming home!
Fritz Now, Thompson. They'll be here soon.

Thompson fades out

> *Fritz and Thompson exit. Jo enters and watches Older Alice*

Older Alice rattles the phone but the line's gone dead

Older Alice (*into the phone to Lilly, the switchboard operator*) Lilly, Lilly? That last caller, can you connect him back through? (*Lilly obviously says no*) I see. ... Yes it was, it was very important. If he should call again, you make sure they find me, you understand? Don't let him go. Tell him ... tell him ... (*She sings*)

No. 23 Tell Him

> Tell him I'll be there.
> I'd meet him anywhere.
> I'd travel all of Europe just to see
> That crooked smile, the twinkle in his eye,
> Tell him by his side is where I want to be.
> Tell him I regret my words when we last met
> Lashing out in anger, haste and fear
> Tell him just to get home now,
> I need him here, I don't care how.
> No matter what it costs I want him here.

Jo That month waiting for your anniversary it must have felt like a lifetime! Did you think he'd show?
Older Alice That was a terrible few weeks for Liverpool. Every night the German bombers rained their fire down on us. Every morning we woke to new scenes of destruction; houses, homes, whole streets reduced to rubble. But I suppose I must have believed in my heart that he was on his way home because that night I gathered everyone together in the ballroom ...

Scene 9

The ballroom at the Adelphi; the past, it's a month later

There is a microphone on a little stage

Older Alice is supervising Brad Finkle and another G.I. who are hoisting up a banner saying "Together Forever". Babs and other staff members are there with G.I.s and a few other Guests

Babs Alice, they say Liverpool's in for another night of bombing.
G.I. The sky's full of storm clouds, should hold 'em off for a while.
An employee That's it! The generator's finally given up.

The Lights dim on the ballroom

Older Alice I don't care, the Adelphi's going to host a celebration tonight, no matter what Mr Hitler throws at us. (*Calling up*) Reg, looks like we will need those storm lanterns.

A bedraggled string of feebly lit storm lanterns fly in. Older Alice moves to the microphone and addresses a crowd of G.I.s, staff and Guests

Ladies and gentlemen, we haven't had much to cheer about recently but tonight we're celebrating romance. They can bomb our homes, our docks and churches but they can't take away our will to survive and our belief in love. Tonight's party is a double celebration, first of all it's always wonderful to hear stories of couples who met here on the dance floor of the Adelphi. A short while ago G.I Brad Finkle stepped out and got a first glance of our very own Babs Barlow and ... well, why don't I let them tell you the rest?

Music out

G.I. Brad Finkle steps gauchley up to the microphone. He has a thick "hay seed" accent

Brad I want to thank all you Liver ... people for the kindnesses you shown me and my buddies since we was stationed here. Only truly beautiful folk could have produced a vision as lovely as my Barbara. Barbara, honey, why don't you come up here and say hi.

Babs joins Brad on the stage

Babs Hi y'all.
Brad Now I'm delighted to announce that last night this adorable creature agreed to be my wife.
Babs Can you believe it, gang. I've finally bagged a Hollywood husband.

Act II, Scene 9   65

Brad (*very good humoured*) Now I've told you, hun, Arkansas ain't so close to Hollywood — but everybody's sure gonna love you down on my pa's chicken farm. (*Crowing like a rooster*) Cock-a-doodle doo!

Babs clucks like a chicken and Brad chases her around to everyone's amusement. They join the crowd listening to Older Alice

A distant rumble of thunder

Older Alice And now, ladies and gentlemen, I have some good news of my own.

The music starts again

Some of you may remember my fiancé or soon to be fiancé left his job here to bravely fight for justice in the Spanish civil war — well, from there we needed him to fight the Nazis and no doubt he's been as troublesome to them as he always was to me ... but, well, I loved him, and I love him still — and I always will and tonight ... well, tonight you'll all see why, because once we made a pact to meet and dance on the roof of the Adelphi Hotel every year on our anniversary, and this year not bombs not storm clouds and certainly not the leaky sink in room 226 is going to stop us.

The air-raid siren sounds

The partygoers start to move off to the air-raid shelters

Babs German bombers are coming.

One of the hotel staff hands Babs a telegram

Male employee Down to the air-raid shelters. Quick everyone, calm and efficient now. Don't forget your gas masks.
Older Alice Wait, come back everyone. It's probably a false alarm.

Eveveryone starts to leave

Babs (*handing Older Alice the telegram*) Telegram for you, Alice.

A roll of thunder

No. 23A "Telegram into Bombing" music starts

Older Alice reads the telegram

Bad news?

Older Alice He's missing in action, presumed dead. No, no! It can't be true.

An explosion in the distance

Babs Oh darlin' ... We'd better get down to the shelters, hun.
Older Alice No, I won't believe it. He'll be there.

Older Alice starts to leave to go to the roof

Babs Where are you going?

Brad prevents Babs chasing after Older Alice

Brad (*pulling Babs towards the shelter*) Come on, honey!
Babs (*calling after her friend in anguish*) Alice!

SCENE 10

The roof of the Adelphi; past and present

Alice confronts Jo in the rain

Older Alice So I climbed up here in the storm. Through the bombs, pitch black most of the way. Sixty years ago tonight. I had to believe. I had to believe that somehow he'd keep his promise.

No. 23A music out

Jo And did he? Did Thompson turn up?
Older Alice I've never stopped hoping, maybe one year. Sometimes you have to wait a long time for a second chance.

Neil arrives with an umbrella

Neil Jo! Jo! I just had an email from my mate. He's done some research on the web. Alice Summers died in an air raid up on this roof in the 1940s.

Older Alice disappears

She's not who she says she is, she's been having you on.

Act II, Scene 10

A roll of thunder

Jo (*quietly to herself*) So that's why she looked so young.

The intro to No 24 Act II Finale starts

Neil You soft git! Whoever it is you've been talking to up here, it's not a woman who died sixty years ago!
Jo Neil?
Neil What?
Jo I'm not waiting sixty years, dance with me.
Neil You what?
Jo I said, dance with me.
Neil But it's pissing down, we'll get soaked.
Jo Do we care?
Neil Are you coming with me?
Jo What do you think? (*She sings*)

No. 24 Act II Finale

> Grab a smile
> They were meant for you and me

Neil You're off your head!

Jo (*singing*)
> Fill your heart up to the brim
> It's true the best things in life are free
>
> Yell if you can
> Laugh when you get a chance
> Sing out that tune in your head
> And always be the first one to dance.

The music swells

The storm lamps, augmented now by many others, burn bright like stars

Jo watches

Older Alice arrives, excited to be meeting Thompson

She looks around for him. And again. She looks at her watch. She looks around for him. She looks. It slowly dawns on her that he isn't coming. She exhales, her excitement draining away

Music out

Silence

Older Alice walks three steps upstage, her back to the audience. On the third step she stops. She senses Thompson is approaching but doesn't look round yet

Thompson entrance music starts

   Older Thompson appears. He pauses. He looks at her, so in love

Thompson Ladybird?
Older Alice You're late.
Thompson Care to dance?

Finally she turns to face him. They are both crying. He takes her in his arms and they dance

Jo is still watching all this. Jo and Neil dance too

Once in a Lifetime (**Reprise**)

   (*Singing*)   The stars are calling out our name
                      It's Liverpool's time again
                      At last the world is waking.

Company (*off*) Ah.

Alice
Jo
Neil
Thompson
          Shout the news across the sky
          Tonight it's you and I
          Who'll choose the road we're taking.

Dancing couples begin to fill up the stage from all directions led by Babs dancing with Roy

                For tonight
                If we dream

Act II, Scene 10

>   The world will dream along with us.
>   We waited long enough, now is the right time.
>   If we fail then we fail but at least we chose to fight
>   Don't waste tonight's
>   Once in a lifetime.
>
> **All**   For tonight
>   If we dream
>   The world will dream along with us.
>   We waited long enough, now is the right time.
>   If we fail then we fail but at least we chose to fight
>   Don't waste tonight's
>   Once in a lifetime.
>   Don't waste tonight's
>   Once in a lifetime

No. 25 First Bows

Curtain calls

Dance for Me Boy: Ensemble
Yippee Ai Eh: Roy and Fritz
Wedding and A Yacht: presenting Babs
First Romances: Delores and Mo present Older Alice
Tell Them: Thompson presenting Jo

> Love like that it never really leaves you
> The years can never pull you two apart
> And though the world can be tough
> It's never rough enough
> That you'll forget love
> The day you let love
> In your heart.

No. 25A Bows Part II

> You can't beat a musical comedy show tune
> A Busby Berkeley matinée.
> Ba ba ba. Da da da da
> When Fred Astaire glides on your spirits soar
> He'll banish all your blues away.
> And soon you're buzzing with the new tune
> (Ah!)

	That's got 'em tapping 'cross the screen. Ba ba. Da da! There's nothing better To the young go-getter Than a full blown Big time Liverpool dance routine.
	Grab a smile They were meant for you and me Fill your heart up to the brim It's true the best things in life are free Yell if you can Laugh when you get a chance
Thompson	Sing out that tune
Older Alice **Jo** }	Sing out that tune
Jo	Sing out that tune
Older Alice **Jo** }	Sing out that tune
All	Sing out that tune in your head And always be the first one up to dance.

Everyone exits to music

THE END

FURNITURE AND PROPERTY LIST

ACT I
Scene 1

On stage: Hotel Reception
Reception front desk. *On it*: phone, pens, etc.

Scene 2

On stage: On the Roof
Nil

Reception Room
Nil

Off stage: Empty bag (**Young Alice**)
Glass (**Lord Rothmore**)

Personal: **Older Alice**: watch
Thompson: 3 wallets, pocket-watch, and numerous other items of "loot" in pockets

Scene 3

On stage: Mo's House
Washing on a line, including a shirt and large sheet
Washing basket

On the Roof
Nil

Hotel Reception
Reception front desk. *On it*: phone, pens, etc.

Personal: **Mo**: clothes pegs

Scene 4

On stage: Hotel Reception
Reception front desk. *On it*: phone, pens, etc.

Hotel Kitchen
Book (for **Fred**)

	On the Roof Nil
Off stage:	Large crate of pots and pans (**Thompson**)
Personal:	**Fritz**: bread in pocket

Scene 5

On stage:	Hotel Entrance Red carpet
	On the Roof Nil
Off stage:	Cameras with 1930s practical flashguns (**Photographers**)

Scene 6

On stage:	Adelphi Ballroom Nil
	On the Roof Nil
Off stage:	Trays of champagne (**Waitresses**) Tray of cigarettes (**Babs**)

Scene 7

On stage:	On the Roof Nil
Off stage:	Rope, or horse (**Hollywood's Roy Rogers**) Bottles of vodka (**Russian Acrobats**) Dog (**Lord Rothmore**)

ACT II
Scene 1

On stage:	On the Roof Nil

Furniture and Property List

Scene 2

On stage: Hotel Reception
Reception front desk. *On it*: phone, pens, etc.

On the Roof
Nil

Off stage: Hollywood magazine (**Babs**)

Personal: **Babs**: compact mirror

Scene 3

On stage: Adelphi Bedroom
Bed

On the Roof
Nil

Personal: **Dolores Gilmore**: wad of cash

Scene 4

On stage: Hotel Reception
Reception front desk. *On it*: phone, pens, etc.

On the Roof
Nil

Scene 5

On stage: On the Roof
Nil

Personal: **Thompson**: engagement ring

Scene 6

On stage: Hotel Reception
Reception front desk. *On it*: phone, pens, etc.

	On the Roof Nil
	Mo's House Nil
Personal:	**Mo**: letter **Neil**: mobile phone

Scene 7

On stage:	Adelphi Ballroom Small stage. *On it*: microphone
	On the Roof Nil

Scene 8

On stage:	Hotel Reception Reception front desk. *On it*: phone, pens, etc.
	In Germany Phone (for **Thompson**)
	On the Roof Nil

Scene 9

On stage:	Adelphi Ballroom Small stage. *On it*: microphone Banner reading "Together Forever" (for **Brad Finkle** and **G.I.**)
	On the Roof Nil
Personal:	**Employee**: telegram

Scene 10

On stage:	On the Roof Nil
Off stage:	Umbrella (**Neil**)

LIGHTING PLOT

Practical fittings required: storm lanterns (ACT II, Scene 9 and Scene 10)

Various interior and exterior settings

PROLOGUE

To open: General lighting

No cues

ACT I

To open: Lighting on **Jo** and **Neil**, dim lighting on hotel roof area

Cue 1	**Neil**: "Battle stations!" *Bring up lighting on front desk*	(Page 1)
Cue 2	At the end of Somebody's on the Roof *Increase lighting on hotel roof area*	(Page 4)
Cue 3	**Older Alice**: (singing) "It seemed like yesterday." *Bring up lighting on hotel reception room in the hotel*	(Page 5)
Cue 4	**Thompson** exits *Focus down on* **Jo** *and* **Older Alice**	(Page 9)
Cue 5	**Older Alice**: " ... tapping in to all that." *Focus down on* **Lord Rothmore** *and* **Guests**	(Page 9)
Cue 6	**Lord Rothmore**: " ... always survive life's setbacks." *Focus down on* **Young Alice** *and* **Thompson**	(Page 9)
Cue 7	**Young Alice**: " And the rest." *Focus down on* **Lord Rothmore** *and* **Guests**	(Page 10)
Cue 8	**Lord Rothmore**: " ... will make us great again." *Focus down on* **Young Alice** *and* **Thompson**	(Page 10)

Cue 9	**Thompson** stares out at the view *Focus down on* **Lord Rothmore** *and* **Guests**	(Page 10)
Cue 10	**Young Alice** bustles back to **Thompson** on the roof *Focus down on* **Young Alice** *and* **Thompson**	(Page 11)
Cue 11	**Thompson** (singing): "Once in a lifetime." *Focus down on* **Lord Rothmore** *and* **Guests**	(Page 12)
Cue 12	**Hotel Staff** stand in attendance *Increase lighting on* **Young Alice**	(Page 12)
Cue 13	At the end of Once in a Lifetime *Lighting on* **Mo**'s *house; dim lighting on the hotel roof*	(Page 13)
Cue 14	**Mo** exits *Fade lighting on* **Mo**'s *house. Bring up lighting on* **Thompson** *and* **Young Alice**	(Page 17)
Cue 15	**Thompson** exits *Concentrate lighting on* **Jo** *and* **Older Alice**	(Page 17)
Cue 16	**Jo**: "... that's what people do to you!" *Crossfade to lighting on* **Neil** *in hotel reception*	(Page 17)
Cue 17	**Neil** exits *Concentrate lighting on* **Jo** *and* **Older Alice** *on roof*	(Page 18)
Cue 18	**Older Alice**: "... mostly low-paid immigrants —" *Bring up lighting on hotel kitchen*	(Page 18)
Cue 19	**All** (singing): "ROUTINE!" *Black-out. When ready bring up lighting on kitchen area,* *with dim lighting on the roof area*	(Page 21)
Cue 20	**Fritz** (singing): "I'll inspire the human race." *Crossfade from kitchen area to hotel reception area*	(Page 23)
Cue 21	**Babs**: "... stake your claim, girl." *Crossfade from hotel reception area to kitchen area*	(Page 23)
Cue 22	**Paddy**: "... should fall in love with." *Crossfade from kitchen area to hotel entrance area*	(Page 25)
Cue 23	**Babs**: "Christ, just a wedding'll do!!" *Crossfade from hotel entrance to ballroom*	(Page 28)
Cue 24	**Hollywood's Roy Rodgers**: "Darn it!" *Fade ballroom lighting; concentrate on roof area*	(Page 35)

Lighting Plot

Cue 25	**Choir**: "Once in a lifetime!" *Fireworks*	(Page 40)

ACT II

To open: Lighting on roof

Cue 26	**Older Alice**: " ... their eyes off him." No.15 intro music *Increase lighting on roof*	(Page 42)
Cue 27	**All** (singing): " ... and accountable to you!" *Decrease lighting on roof; bring up lighting on hotel reception area*	(Page 45)
Cue 28	**Frank** and **Thompson** exit. **Babs** enters *Crossfade from hotel reception to spot on **Babs***	(Page 47)
Cue 29	**Thompson** enters another area *Spot on **Thompson***	(Page 47)
Cue 30	No. 17 Bedroom Underscore *Cut spots and bring up lighting on an Adelphi bedroom*	(Page 48)
Cue 31	**Delores Gilmore**: "Lucky someone." *Crossfade from bedroom to hotel reception*	(Page 50)
Cue 32	**Lord Rothmore** leaves *Fade lighting on hotel reception; increase lighting on roof*	(Page 52)
Cue 33	**Young Alice**: (singing) "That may break my heart in two." *Fade to black-out*	(Page 55)
Cue 34	**Babs**, **Lily** and **Rose** enter *Bring up lighting on hotel reception; dim lighting on roof*	(Page 55)
Cue 35	No. 19B segues into underscoring *Crossfade from hotel reception to Mo's house*	(Page 57)
Cue 36	**Young Alice** opens the letter and begins to read *Spot on **Thompson***	(Page 57)
Cue 37	**Young Alice** (singing): " ... the first one up to dance!" *Cut spot on **Thompson**; crossfade from **Mo**'s house to hotel reception*	(Page 59)
Cue 38	**Babs**: "... on the dance floor again." *Crossfade from hotel reception to Adelphi ballroom*	(Page 60)

Cue 39	**Older Alice** picks up the phone *Crossfade from ballroom to hotel reception; bring up lighting on* **Older Thompson**	(Page 62)
Cue 40	**Older Alice**: "… everyone together in the ballroom …" *Crossfade from hotel reception and* **Older Thompson** *to the ballroom*	(Page 63)
Cue 41	**An Employee**: " … finally given up." *Dim lighting on ballroom area*	(Page 64)
Cue 42	**Older Alice**: "… we will need those storm lanterns." *Fly in practicals*	(Page 64)
Cue 43	**Babs**: "Alice!" *Fade on ballroom; concentrate lighting on roof*	(Page 66)
Cue 44	**Jo** (singing): "And always be the first one up to dance." *Augment and increase lighting level of practicals*	(Page 67)

EFFECTS PLOT

ACT I

Cue 1	The Lights come up on an area of the kitchen *Blast of steam*	(Page 21)
Cue 2	**Choir**: "Once in a lifetime!" *Fireworks*	(Page 40)

ACT II

Cue 3	To open ACT II *Sound of wind*	(Page 41)
Cue 4	**All**: " ... and accountable to you!" *Sounds of hotel reception; continue throughtout Scene 2*	(Page 45)
Cue 5	**Brad** chases **Babs** around *Distant rumble of thunder*	(Page 65)
Cue 6	**Older Alice**: " ... is going to stop us." *Air-raid siren*	(Page 65)
Cue 7	**Babs**: "Telegram for you, Alice." *Roll of thunder*	(Page 65)
Cue 8	**Older Alice**: " It can't be true." *Explosion in distance*	(Page 66)
Cue 9	**Babs**: "Alice!" *Sound of rain*	(Page 66)
Cue 10	**Neil**: " ... she's been having you on." *Roll of thunder*	(Page 66)

www.ingramcontent.com/pod-product-compliance
Ingram Content Group UK Ltd.
Pitfield, Milton Keynes, MK11 3LW, UK
UKHW021837210426
5322IPUK00021B/335